Village of the Outcasts

Village
of the Outcasts

ROBERT M. WULFF

FOREWORD BY HUBERT H. HUMPHREY

Vice President of the United States

DOUBLEDAY & COMPANY, INC.

Garden City, New York

1967

Library of Congress Catalog Card Number 66–15441
Copyright © 1966 by Robert M. Wulff
All Rights Reserved
Printed in the United States of America
First Edition

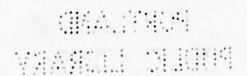
R. M.

ACKNOWLEDGMENTS

It will be obvious to the reader that this book could not have come about without the assistance, love, and understanding of countless people. My gratitude to all is unbounded.

I want especially to thank Ken Methold, my longtime friend in Chiengmai. An English author with numerous books and articles to his credit, he worked long hours putting order and readability into my scattered diary accounts and taped reminiscences. Ken, like me, is married to a lovely Thai girl and fully appreciates the joys and the difficulties such a union creates. His empathy and his literary skills were indispensable to the creation of this book.

A word of thanks must also be included for Evelyn Metzger of Doubleday, who put in far more than the normal time and effort in editing the manuscript. Without the interest and initiative of Mrs. Metzger and Bill Connell, Assistant to Vice President Humphrey, my diaries might never have been transformed into this book.

My debt to Mr. Connell extends far beyond the book. His encouragement and his many representations on behalf of our projects in Thailand more than once made the difference between failure and success.

To Vice President Hubert Humphrey I want to express my humble appreciation for his kindness and personal concern and for his inspiration to me. He is truly interested in ordinary people and our problems.

My friend Ray Hemenway has been a source of strength and support

v

367209

B
W961

3567 Pub 3.17

and has played an important part in the shaping of my story. I am deeply grateful to him.

My mother and father gave me the kind of support for which there are no adequate words of appreciation. When others would have advised me to give up, they kept encouraging me. How can I ever fully acknowledge such faith and love?

Ajana, my wife, has played the most vital part of the last half of this story and can never be praised enough to satisfy my feelings. Her parents, Dr. and Mrs. Arie S. Watana, have also been pillars of support. I cannot thank them enough for the pleasures of Thai family life they so generously share with me.

My friends in Thailand are almost too numerous to list. It will be apparent to the reader that Surin was as responsible for the success of this story as I. My other dear friends from the New Life Foundation and from the Department of Public Welfare and the Ministry of Interior all deserve special thanks.

The list of acknowledgments could go on and on, mentioning nearly every person in the book. This is as it should be, however, because this is a story not alone of my experiences but of contacts and associations with many splendid people.

ROBERT M. WULFF

FOREWORD

Meeting Robert Wulff for the first time, one would not suspect that this tall, quiet, rather shy young man has already lived a more adventurous, richer, and more productive life than most Americans enjoy in a lifetime. He is a man who looks very much like the high school teacher which he might have become, and for which he was trained back in Minnesota. But the nature of Bob Wulff is more like one part missionary, one part mountain man, and one part Yankee whaler.

You would like Bob and his strikingly lovely wife, Ajana. In the pages of his account, drawn heavily from his diaries, you will get to know a good deal about them. It is a marvelous story, one that cannot help making you prouder to be an American, more appreciative of what we have here in America, and more determined that much more can be done to help our fellow men.

Late in the 1950s, when I first began speaking publicly about an American Peace Corps, I was drawing on my knowledge of a number of experiments by individuals and groups of Americans and British. The admirable International Voluntary Services, for example, was doing a pathbreaking job of putting Western skills to work to help people help themselves. The IVS volunteers are still hard at work, by the way, in South Vietnam and other countries. But I also had brought to my attention the work of a number of individuals. One was Bob Wulff.

vii

Bob has been a true pioneer. He had the wanderlust, and some deep inner drive that called him into the wilderness. And he had that sense of mission that has caught up so many Americans through the generations—men and women who have given up comfort and position to go and work with the hungry, the diseased, and the ignorant.

What training did he have to help the crippled and disfigured people with whom he chose to work? Where did he learn to build irrigation systems, housing developments, roads, and bridges? Where did he learn to drive elephants? Who taught him how to lead despairing outcasts into a new life, to design their tools, to be successful farmers and artisans?

The truth, apparently, is that a typical American, from a typical American small town with a typical American education, is the unknowing possessor of a fantastic heritage. What took Bob Wulff to Thailand in the first place you will have to judge for yourself in reading his book. But it is clear that Bob carried with him to Thailand a tradition of inventiveness and ingenuity, an acquaintance with tools and mechanics, and a vast storehouse of knowledge that we take for granted but which is priceless in the backwoods of the world.

Bob has finished one phase of his work in Thailand. Now he is in the training section of the Peace Corps. He is still hard at work —teaching, leading, bringing to bear his warm and good heart, and his remarkable versatility in the cause of victory over human misery.

He has been too generous to us who gave him some small help along the way. What he was willing to do, what human misery he was willing to face, what horrors he fought, few of us would have been willing to take on. It was his strength and courage and determination, and those of his Thai friends, that won their battle.

I am proud to know Bob Wulff. He is truly a soldier of the Lord—a healer, a builder, a leader. And yet—and this is perhaps the most encouraging aspect of all—Bob Wulff is not unique among Americans, though he took a lonelier and grimmer path than most. There are many thousands who have volunteered to help others help themselves. Practicing the peaceful arts of teaching and healing, men and women from America have spread throughout the world. Like Bob Wulff, they have brought not only help to the unfortunate, but also honor to their families, their communities, and their country.

HUBERT H. HUMPHREY
Vice President of the United States

Village of the Outcasts

Chapter 1

It is not easy to know what to do with one's life. Most of us, I think, drift into a job without giving it too much thought. Either our path is carefully laid out for us by our parents or, if we have a reasonable education behind us, we take up a profession because it offers security and a foreseeable future. Then when it is too late to retrace our steps and start off in something different we spend half our time fretting because we think we are in the wrong job.

I did not want this to happen to me, and although I had a fairly good idea of the kind of work I wanted to do when I left high school I did not want to commit myself too soon. It is necessary to go into these details of my background because people are always asking me how it came about that I started working with leprosy patients in the jungle of Northern Thailand. I think they expect me to answer that I have a vocation for this work and that I knew many years ago that this is what I would be doing today. Nothing could be further from the truth. I hoped that I would find something worthwhile to do with my life but I had no idea that things would turn out as they have. However, at the same time I believe that in some way unknown to me God has directed me into rehabilitation work. I know that for years in my prayers I asked for help and guidance. I can hear myself murmuring as a teen-ager, "Please God help me to find something worthwhile to do." I like to think that my prayers have been answered.

Getting down the events of the past twelve years on paper has made me think about myself more than ever before. I have tried to understand why I have said and done things. Perhaps the conclusions I have come to are worth writing down, not because they are of importance, but because they suggest that it is not necessary to be a "good" person, a missionary, or even a doctor to do something of value for other people. It has seemed to me that there are two contradictory traits in my character. There is my religious belief on the one hand which has led me in to social work—"do-gooding," if you like. On the other hand there is the slightly devil-may-care spirit of the adventurer, the wandering bum, that got me to Asia in the first place and which, incidentally, nearly led me into a currency-smuggling racket in the Philippines. This kind of crime and building villages with leprosy patients are rather far apart, but the fact that I considered both makes me think that it is not necessary to be wholly "good" to be of value. I like to think that there are thousands of Americans just like me who would be willing to come out to the developing nations but are held back because they cannot think of themselves as social workers. I am hoping that this book will encourage them to forget their doubts or their sense of being the wrong kind of person. Very often the wrong kind of person turns out to be of more value to a project than the man or woman with the more acceptable motivation. The tough guys often get a great deal more done than their "holier" compatriots. Very often it is sheer stubbornness or conceit that forces one to overcome a difficult situation. I should like to be able to say that it is my religious faith that has enabled me to overcome obstacles. In some instances this would be true, but in many others it has been what my English friends call "simple bloody mindedness." Sometimes I try to justify my pig-headedness by thinking that it is God's way of working through me, but I should hate to have to argue this point with a theologian!

When I graduated from high school in Albert Lea, Minnesota,

in 1944, I had vague ideas of becoming a teacher or doing social work with juvenile delinquents. I also considered going into law or politics and daydreamed of becoming a senator or something. My home life had been a really happy one and I suppose I felt I wanted to work with kids less fortunate than myself or achieve something that would make my folks proud of me. But the immediate thing I wanted to do was to join the Army. My brother was in the Pacific, where he had been in combat with the First Marine Division, and his letters home were full of his experiences. I felt it was rather unfair that he should have done and seen so much that I could experience only secondhand. The war was practically over by then, of course, but I was determined that I should have a share of it, if only at the tail end. This is not to suggest that I like war, but I was just eighteen and rightly or wrongly, I was stirred by the excitement of it. Also, I did not like the idea very much of being overshadowed by my brother.

Three or four months after graduation I was inducted into the Navy and sent to Great Lakes. Nine days later I was discharged on the grounds that my eyesight was not good enough. This was humiliating, for I can see perfectly well with glasses, thick though the lenses may be. I tried the Merchant Marine, but could not get into that either. Then I nagged the Army to draft me but they were not interested in me. As all the armed forces seemed closed to me I decided to forget the whole idea and I enrolled in a prelaw course at the University of Minnesota. A few months later, just as I was settling down and had gone out for football, the Army informed me that yes, they would take me after all.

After various intelligence tests I was moved about from base to base doing such high-grade work as emptying wastepaper baskets. This was not the kind of military experience I had looked forward to and I remember that I fussed and fretted about it and in my immature way appealed to God in my prayers to get me into something better. I offered God a bargain. If He would get me shipped to China, I said, I promised that I would do whatever work He directed me to. He only had to show me the way and I would take it.

I realized that I was asking a lot because at that time there were no postings for U.S. forces in China. Nevertheless I felt that China was the country to ask for. I knew very little about it, only the odd stories heard from missionaries who gave occasional talks at the local Lutheran church. But I was attracted to the idea of China—its people and centuries of civilization.

A few days later it was announced that a shipment of a hundred and twenty fellows had been selected for assignments in China. I was one of them. Although I was excited I was also worried. I had made this bargain, and whether or not it could be proved that my assignment was an answer to my prayers, it seemed to me that I was now bound to take up some kind of missionary work when my service was over. I did not like the idea at all. I had never wanted to be an ordained missionary or even a doctor but now it seemed that I would have to do one of these two things. I decided to put off even thinking about it until I had to make a decision, by which time I might have found a way round the dilemma.

As things turned out, going to China solved the problem for me. I had not been in the country long before I realized that I could not turn my back on all the misery and poverty of the Chinese people. I could not go back home after my service, forget all about what I had seen, and settle in some safe two-car, split-level life in Albert Lea. I felt that there had to be something that even I could do to help them.

I was fortunate in that my work in the Army gave me a lot of travel and the time to wander the streets and get the feel of Chinese life. I was a courier, taking mail from headquarters to peace teams. These teams were made up of a few officers, a radio operator, a driver, and an odd-job private. They operated in China under some arrangement that I never fully understood. The organization was never explained to me and I suspect even now that the peace teams had no official standing. At that time American policy toward China was influenced by the Institute of Pacific Relations, a group that was later exposed as a Communist "front" organization. However, few if any of us knew this at the time and we simply carried out our orders which were to move from trouble spot to trouble spot and attempt to mediate between Chiang Kai-shek's Kuomintang forces and Mao Tse-tung's Communists, who were both busily engaged in killing one another off. Basically the idea was that the Chinese people should be persuaded to stop their pointless civil war and adopt a fine old American two-party system. In view of the economic condition of China at the time, this was a pretty naïve policy.

In fact, American policy toward China disturbed me—not only because it seemed unwise, but also because it was causing the Chinese people real hardship. Under an agreement made between Roosevelt and Stalin (over the opposition of Churchill) the Chinese people had been forced to supply Russia with certain raw materials. As a result of this agreement their country had been stripped of everything industrially useful. Before the war, for example, the Japanese had installed in Manchuria one of the largest steel mills in the world. When I went to see it, there was practically nothing left of it. The whole thing had been dismantled and sent to Russia.

Most of Manchuria's coal was going to Russia, and it was pathetic to see Chinese people freezing to death because they had no fuel. The railway yards were haunted by scores of men, women, and children sifting through the ashes and clinkers from the steam engines for something that could be mixed with dirt and burned to produce a little heat.

Never a day went by without my passing starving people who were so weak that they simply lay down in the street and waited for death. And yet among all this misery one could see and feel the indomitable spirit of the Chinese people. I saw them trotting

5

down the streets carrying the most tremendous loads but smiling and apparently happy. They asked for so little from life—a little food, a little warmth, and the happiness that comes from a good family life. It seemed to me then that America, instead of lightening their burdens, was adding to them. I felt guilty and rather ashamed of what we were doing. No doubt we meant well but our actions were having a tragic effect.

And, of course, we could not even begin to achieve our purpose. Pressure would be brought on Chiang Kai-shek's men to stop fighting in a given area. For a time there would be a lull, but during the cease-fire the Communist forces would regroup and nibble back here and there small pieces of territory they had lost.

I had not been in China long before I became friendly with a group of eight refugees in Changchun. At one time they had all been medical students. When I met them they were working as coolies in the kitchens of our billet. One of them, Wong Teh Kung, spoke excellent English and managed to get himself taken on as an interpreter. He had been a paratrooper with the Kuomintang forces during World War II and had been educated in Japanese schools in Manchuria, so he spoke not only Chinese and English, but Japanese and Russian. He was a remarkable man and I spent hours listening to him tell me about China.

He was the leader—the protector—of the little group. He was the only one with a regular job, and the other seven lived off his wages. They had managed to find an empty house that belonged to a relative and had moved in. There was no furniture: Wong's wages could not buy furniture as well as food for eight hungry young men.

But as the months passed things became a little easier for them. Han Lio got a job in a bank and this almost doubled their standard of living: they could eat every day. And from time to time the others would pick up a day's work and pool what they earned. Wong Teh Kung suggested that I teach them all English. This seemed an excellent idea and we started regular classes. Slowly their English improved and it was possible for me to get to know them better. Whereas previously they had been little more than pleasant Chinese faces, now, for me, their individual personalities emerged. One of them, Wong Chen Tang, became an even closer friend than his namesake, Wong Teh Kung. Wong Chen Tang eventually became a doctor and so to avoid confusion, I will refer to him as Dr. Wong. He became largely responsible for my return to Asia, and many years later he came to Thailand and worked with me in our first rehabilitation village.

I spent most of my time with my new Chinese friends. They took me out sightseeing and explained to me the background of famous buildings, ceremonies, and Chinese customs. I tried to learn Chinese but found it very difficult, and, anyway, my friends really preferred to practice their English on me.

I saw many unforgettable things in China. In particular I saw too much death. Until I left home, death had no horror for me. It was always concealed in an ornate casket in a luxurious funeral parlor. In China at that time death was everywhere in the streets. The bodies were carried to the edge of the town and dumped into ditches. Perhaps I was too impressionable and let my feelings become too involved with the plight of these people. I do not know. But at that time the behavior of most of the other U.S. forces disgusted me. In the midst of all the misery and starvation many of them could find nothing better to do than get drunk in brothels and goad the rickshaw boys and coolies into fights. The Americans always won, not because they were tough, but because the Chinese did not want to offend the free-spending American forces. It was not my idea of sport to pay a man for the privilege of beating him up. Neither could I understand the satisfaction the fellows got from making use of girls who had to sell their bodies if their families were to eat. There was no dignity in it for anyone concerned, and I think it was witnessing the terrible indignity of man that later determined that I should work with lepers, men

7

and women so disfigured and feared that they are shunned and rejected by most communities.

Although during my Army service I contributed nothing to the plight of the Chinese people except sympathy and friendship, which is hardly of much value to people dying in the streets from cold, hunger, and disease, I tried to prolong my assignment. But the Army was not interested in providing draftees with overseas sightseeing tours, and I was informed that an extension of my assignment was out of the question unless I signed on as a regular for a three-year engagement. Suspecting that if I signed, military bureaucracy would promptly assign me to Alaska or some other area far away from China, I declined the invitation and became a civilian again.

Back in my home town, I talked and talked about my experiences. In terms of action they were very tame, but to me the everyday life of the Chinese people was fascinating. I fear I became a great bore and that only my mother and father believed what I told them.

I was by this time convinced that there was some kind of work for me in Asia, preferably in China. I also knew, however, that I had to have something to offer. Good intentions are not enough. Unfortunately I was not attracted to medicine and I still had no vocation to enter God's ministry. Although my religion gave me great comfort and I hoped that others could also be led to find strength and joy through Christianity, I did not have and still do not have much evangelical fervor. Having rejected the life of a missionary or a doctor, I looked around for some other way of equipping myself for a useful return to Asia. A training in education and sociology seemed a sensible choice and so I withdrew from the university and put aside all thoughts of law or politics and transferred to St. Olaf College. This large Christian college, with its fine buildings, well-established academic reputation, and national fame for choral music, had on its staff a number of men who had had experience of mission work overseas. Some of the faculty had been in China, and I felt that my ideas would probably receive a sympathetic hearing.

But my years in college were not really satisfactory. The course was no more than a means to an end for me, and I was itching to get back to China. The scramble for good grades that occupied the other students did not interest me. I am afraid I drifted through college with only the sociology lectures and field work making much impression on me. I played some football but the competitive spirit that had driven me to play a hard game in high school seemed to have faded. The only things that really interested me were reading books on China in the college library and running a movie business that I had started. The business was making a lot of money for me. It enabled me to live well at college and to save up for my return to China.

I had started this movie business in the months between my discharge from the Army and the beginning of the new academic year at St. Olaf. At first I had worked as a janitor in a print shop to fill in the time and earn a little pocket money. Then I got in touch with a lady who ran a small business showing outdoor movies in the country towns. She had lost interest in running the business and let me rent her equipment. On fine nights I set up a screen, showed a few films, and sold popcorn. These performances were sponsored by local tradesmen who wanted to promote their businesses. There were a number of other groups doing the same kind of thing, but I studied their mistakes and fairly soon the organization grew and I had people working for me. It was lucrative. It was also educational. I learned about business, and from watching movies night after night, I picked up a degree of moviemaking technique. I soon bought my own movie camera. A few years later I was able to use this camera to make a film on leprosy in Thailand. If it had not been for my movie business I would never have had the money to return to Asia, or the equipment and technique to make the movie.

During wintertime, of course, I could do nothing with the business, but as soon as the summer vacation started I was on the road again. I cannot remember exactly how much I saved but it was several thousand dollars.

But I still had no real plan for my future. I had no clear idea of what I was going to do or how I should do it. Then, toward the end of my third year at St. Olaf, I had a letter from Dr. Wong. Mainland China was by then a Communist nation, and so he had settled in Nationalist China's Formosa. He wanted me to join him when I finished college. He was sure there was something I could do. He did not say what but he gave me the impression that as soon as I was actually in Formosa some kind of work would materialize. When I told people that I intended to go to Formosa they thought I was crazy. What, they wanted to know, could I possibly do out there? As I did not know, I suggested that I might join the Nationalist Army. A few months later I did, in fact, volunteer, but the Chinese Consul in Manila advised me against doing anything so foolish, and fortunately I took his advice.

And so, when I had completed my course and got my B.A. degree, I did one more season in the movie-showing business, turned my money into traveler's checks, packed a couple of bags, and on April 23, 1952, left San Francisco Harbor on board the M.S. *Francisville*, bound for Manila.

"May God," I wrote in my diary that night, "favor my travels."

Chapter 2

The voyage to Manila was pleasant but I was too excited and uncertain about my future with Wong in Formosa to really enjoy the long, slow days. The morning after we landed I went straight to the Chinese Consulate to obtain my visa for Formosa. The Consul looked through my passport and frowned.

"I am very sorry, Mr. Wulff, but there is an entry here specifically restricting you from going to Formosa."

"What!"

"I am sorry, but yes. You can see for yourself." And he pointed to a small stamp that I had not noticed. When you apply for a passport to go to a given country you hardly expect the officials to deliberately prevent you from going there.

"There must be a mistake."

"Yes, I am sure it is a mistake. I have never seen this restriction before."

"What do I do?"

"It will be a simple matter. Go to your own consulate here and ask them to cancel the restriction. Then I can issue your visa." He smiled, and surprised but not too alarmed, I went off to the U.S. Consulate.

Unfortunately, at that time a large number of junior officials in the U.S. Foreign Service did not appear to have any clear idea of their responsibilities. Or perhaps the misunderstanding was mine.

In any event, my experience was that they were not interested in the problems of their own countrymen and that they tended to develop an exaggerated idea of their own importance.

I told my story.

"There is nothing we can do about this. The whole matter must be referred to Washington."

"But I want to go to Formosa next week."

"Mr. Wulff, if Washington has put this restriction on, Washington must take it off. It is really quite simple. Do you want me to forward your complaint or don't you?"

"Yes," I said, "I do."

The clerk—I refuse to believe she held a higher grade—promised me she would have a reply in about three months.

I could not accept that having come so far I would be denied entry to Formosa. I could not understand the purpose of the restrictions. Why had the U.S. Government decided that I must not enter Formosa? What had I done or not done, I asked myself, that made me such a special threat? There was nothing. The restriction had to be a mistake and if I could find a helpful official there might be a way of getting round it.

I returned to the Chinese Consul and told him my story—the whole story. He was most sympathetic. When I mentioned that I had considered joining the Nationalist Army he became almost paternal but put forward a hundred good reasons for not joining. He did not appear to doubt my sincerity, although I realize now that he must have thought me very odd.

The best advice he gave me was to fly to Hong Kong, where, he suggested, a different set of American officials might look at my problem in a different way. This seemed a sensible suggestion. However, before leaving the Philippines I wanted to see a little more of the country, so I decided to stay on for another week, before going on to Hong Kong.

When I read through the diary I kept on my travels I come

across a number of remarks that make me shudder at my naïveté and immaturity. It is difficult to believe that I could have been so unrealistic. What did I think I was doing? How could I possibly have imagined, even for a minute, that I would find myself useful work to do? I knew nothing and I knew nobody. I was no more than a wandering bum with vague ideas. I was also very lonely and not a little scared in Manila. The city was full of small-time gangsters, pimps, and prostitutes, and all visitors were clearly warned not to walk down back streets after dark. Every day the newspapers headlined holdups, shootings, and other violence. The Filipinos seemed to be surly and all on the make, and Manila was a far cry from the small Chinese country towns I had got to know so well during my Army service.

I was also disappointed by the absence of an Oriental culture in Manila. It was the Orient I wanted to work in, not an Asian Brooklyn. Two extracts from my diary sum up my impressions at that time.

May 15, 1952, Manila

Manila is a maze of confusion and congestion. Eighty per cent of the shops are run by Chinese of which there are about a hundred thousand in Manila alone. Most of the buildings are small and filthy with only an occasional beautiful structure here and there. Of course, many ruins of buildings damaged during the war are still reaching up their crumbling walls into the sky. People are scurrying everywhere. Peddlers are selling everything. Small children are running around naked. Small jeep-buses and trucks are piling up traffic jams on every available narrow street. Large Catholic cathedrals are swarming with beggars and people selling candles and veils. Oriental music mixed with American jukebox records blares from various different shops. In some sections the smell is very noticeable but it is not so bad as I had expected. But

13

the worst thing of all is that too many natives look to me as if they want to cut my throat. I am sure this is my imagination and that I am being unfair, but what a relief it is when somebody smiles. I hope that in a few days I shall get accustomed to seeing dark faces and they will begin to appear a little more civil and friendly. It does not seem to be taking much on this trip to make me homesick. What a big, brave world traveler I am!

May 18, 1952, Baguio

So far the Philippines have been a little disappointing to me. They are of course part of the Orient and yet something of the full flavor is missing. There is the same odor in the air and the same sense of poverty and confusion but there is something lacking. I have decided that American and Western influence is responsible. Oriental architecture and temples are rarely seen. Instead of seeing a beautiful temple on the top of a mountain, you can see only a church steeple. I guess I should be glad that Christianity has made such progress on the islands, but when I look at the ceremonies and the vendors selling candles and veils and flowers and images of the saints around the large Catholic churches and cathedrals, I wonder just how pure this Christianity is. It seems too bad that the coming of Christianity should have to change the entire flavor of a civilization, but I guess it is necessary. Oriental religions are responsible for nearly all the different architectures of the East as well as the little peculiar superstitious mannerisms and customs. And I guess that if the religions disappear the other effects just naturally disappear also. I realize that Christianity should not compromise but there is something so completely different and beautiful about Oriental culture that it is a shame it has to go. The more I see and learn the more I understand the attitude of the East in calling Western culture cold and crude. My thoughts seem to be bordering along dangerous lines and yet I cannot help wondering.

I was now beginning to have vague doubts about the feasibility of my trip, and I suspected that I might never get to Formosa. Therefore I decided that I would have to settle for a tourist's life before returning home. Accordingly, I got visas for Siam, Burma, and India. In actual fact I did not require a visa for Siam (now officially renamed Thailand) as Americans are granted special privileges there. Indeed, my visit to the Siamese Consul was one of the few bright spots of my stay in Manila. Siamese people have all the charm and courtesy of the Chinese plus what I can only describe as a greater physical beauty. The eyes and smile of Siamese men and women are the greatest heart-softeners that I know.

But before I left Manila I almost fell a victim to another kind of charm. I met an American hardware salesman in the hotel. He was a very smooth talker and an unusually sympathetic listener. I poured out to him all my frustration over the restriction in my passport, and we sat for hours complaining about the government in general and its overseas officials in particular. I was feeling in a rebellious mood and my disappointments and grievances were almost strong enough to overcome my ideals. If I was going to be prevented from helping others, I felt, then I would help myself instead. I was in a petulant mood.

The hardware salesman, realizing how ripe I was for exploitation, told me about his currency-smuggling activities. As an accredited businessman he could obtain visas for most countries without trouble, and he doubled his income by smuggling currency into these countries and selling it on the black market. But there was a limit to the amount of currency that could be safely secreted on his person. If, he suggested, we worked together we could both make a good living, if not our fortunes. Would I be interested in working with him?

I should prefer to say that I rejected the proposal with high-minded indignation, but this would not be true. I felt that as I had been prevented by the government from reaching my destination, it would be no crime to try to get back some of the money I had spent. I know now that this was specious reasoning, but at the time I was feeling very low and depressed and disgruntled. I told him I would think about it. In some ways the idea appealed to me. I had come out looking for adventure and assumed I would find it in social work with Dr. Wong. Now that this possibility was becoming more remote I was ready to consider adventure of a different kind.

But, fortunately, my scruples were still functioning sufficiently well to keep me out of trouble, and the next morning I told the hardware man that I had decided against the idea. A few hours later I packed my bags and caught a plane to Hong Kong.

When I arrived in Hong Kong it was too late to go to the Consulate. The next day was a Saturday and the Consulate would be closed. It would also be closed on Sunday and on Monday, which was a local holiday. So I had three more days to fill before I could take another step toward Formosa. I spent them sight-seeing in Hong Kong and Macao and spent nearly all my money on presents for friends and relations at home. This was foolish, but anyone who has visited Hong Kong will understand how serious the temptations are.

At last, on the following Tuesday, I went to the U.S. Consulate. The staff were far more courteous than in Manila, but their answer was the same. There was nothing they could do. Washington had put the restriction on. Washington would have to take it off. I was back where I started.

I had, of course, written to Dr. Wong weeks before, telling him to expect me. Now I had to cable him and tell him that I could not get to him. But could he, I asked, get to me? It seemed such a shame for me to have come so far without having at least a brief meeting with him. He cabled back that he would like to come to Hong Kong but that his own government would not give him an exit permit, and without this he could not get a visa for Hong Kong. I thought this was totally disgraceful. Here were two friends who wanted nothing more than to meet, and yet for reasons known only to themselves their respective governments had the authority to forbid such a meeting. We were caught up in a tangle of red tape which could not be unraveled.

Everything, it seemed, had gone wrong. I had spent most of my money and achieved nothing. There was nothing else for me to do except to go home via Thailand, Burma, and India with my presumptuous tail between my legs. Even more disturbing to me than the sense of failure was the fear that either the call to do good work had been self-deception or I had proved myself unworthy. I had been a big-headed fool, and now I was being taught a lesson.

I cabled home for a little more money and flew to Bangkok. Then, I thought, off to Rangoon and Calcutta and home to a tourist's return. But I got no farther than Siam.

Most of the story that follows took place in Thailand, and so perhaps I may be forgiven if I include here my impressions of Bangkok recorded in my diary when I first came to Thailand in 1952.

June 7, 1952

This morning I toured by boat through the canals that crisscross this city and visited one of the larger temples. The tour was wonderful and defies adequate description. Much of Bangkok and its twin city across the river, Thonburi, is laid out with connecting canals instead of streets. These canals run out into the country and on them much of the city's trade is carried on. Nearly everything is sold on small boats so that the people living on the canal-banks and on the canals themselves need wait only for the right boat to come by to purchase all the things they need. The people do not have to leave their homes. Naturally, these canals are teeming with activity. In addition to these floating stores there are many kinds of light industry carried on along the canalbanks. Most of the small factories are located right on the banks and the canals are used for transporting their raw materials and products. Every domestic function is also carried on in full sight of the canal. As the climate is so warm, most houses consist of little more than floors elevated on poles above the water, with grass-thatched roofs to keep off the rain. The walls are usually grass mats that can be rolled up to let in any breeze during the day. All aspects of the family life are in public view. The people go about in all sorts of dress and undress, and cook their meals and attend to bodily functions with complete indifference to the fact that they are always in sight of dozens of other people. This often strikes Americans as being dirty and immodest, until they get to know the living conditions and the climate. We Americans are probably rather silly about the personal aspects of our existence. It is almost as if we feel that each individual is made and functions differently from the next.

After we had spent some time going up and down these canals we stopped to see the royal barges. These are the boats that are used to carry the King on his rare public appearances. I was told that the main boat for the King is about one hundred and seventy feet long and about twelve feet wide at the widest part. The boats are long and graceful with huge carved and inlaid figures forming the bows and the sterns. Eighty oarsmen are needed to paddle the royal barge, with alternate oarsmen having silver- and gold-painted paddles. The entire boat is inlaid with pieces of mirror to reflect the light. A large jeweled throne, about ten feet high, is fastened on to the royal barge for the King to sit on. The barges are on racks in the boathouse now, but I can imagine what a dazzling and colorful spectacle they must make when in use. There are also seven other large barges besides the royal one, and these are used to carry priests and high officials.

After looking at the barges we stopped at the Temple of the Dawn. This is an immense and impressive place. The temple grounds must cover several acres. Spread over this area are the meeting places, the priests' living quarters, and many small statues of the Buddha, each in a small temple. But the most eye-catching and significant feature of the temple is a huge *prang* or tower that stands in the center of the area. This tower rises to an approximate height of two hundred and fifty feet. The base is probably two hundred feet square and is surrounded by four smaller towers each of about a hundred feet in height. This main tower has an outside stairway on each of the four sides, which climbs to about a hundred feet. At about every twenty-five feet, there is a walk all around the tower. Each succeeding flight of stairs gets steeper and narrower.

June 8, 1952

Last night I went to a Siamese theater to watch a performance of *Saming Phra Ram Volunteering to Fight,* an episode from the Raja Thiraj. The performance was interesting but also rather long. The production ran for just over three hours without a single pause or intermission. I had a seat in the front row and so did not miss a thing. I had read the story of the play before I went so that I could follow what was happening. The cast must have numbered about a hundred persons including the orchestra and the group readers. The orchestra consisted entirely of Siamese instruments which resembled types of marimbas and xylophones and boxlike violins. The music was quite unusual but it set the mood of the action very effectively. Most of the dialogue was read by a group of readers sitting with the orchestra, but in certain scenes the dialogue was spoken by the actors on the stage. It was a peculiar arrangement that I did not fully understand. Some scenes were acted and spoken like a Western play, but then would come scenes in which the play was in pantomime and the dialogue was spoken by the readers rather like the chorus in Greek drama. Most of the parts were played by girls, including the lead, but the comic-relief parts were all played by men. There were long stretches of slapstick comedy in some scenes. It was amusing to see what I had always thought of as American humor being performed by Asian actors. The costumes and sets were all very impressive and they indicated to me something of the difference between Chinese and Siamese culture.

The play finished at about eleven-fifteen and I had a pleasant ride back to the hotel by *samlor* (a three-wheel bicycle taxi) through the dark and now deserted city. The ride took over half an hour and it was peaceful to ride through the city when it was asleep.

June 9, 1952

Last night I really saw something. I went to the weekly Siamese boxing show at the National Arena. It seems that Siamese-style boxing is the national sport here and the people follow it as we do baseball. There are many boxing clubs in the city where fighters can train. The arena was one of the finest little boxing arenas I have ever seen. It is round so that there are no bad corner seats in the balcony. It probably holds between five to ten thousand fans. The ring is built on lines similar to U.S. specifications and the referee, judges, timekeepers, and seconds are all similar to those used in international-style boxing. But there the similarity between Siamese and Western boxing comes to an abrupt end. Before the fighters enter the ring and immediately upon entering, they perform religious prayers and gestures. They kneel on the floor, prostrate themselves and kow tow, and make various kinds of genuflections. Then they listen to the referee's instructions and go to their corners to await the bell. When the bell rings a small orchestra begins to play weird music. The orchestra consists of two tom-toms, a kind of clarinet, and bells. This orchestra plays throughout the fight and is intended to stir the fighters on to even greater efforts. As the action gets faster the music gets faster, and vice versa.

The fighters wear regulation boxing gloves but are barefoot and they have a special kind of bandage wrapped around their ankles and the arches of their feet. They also usually wear a small arm-band on one arm as a religious or good-luck charm. The rules permit not only regular punching, but the use of rabbit punches, backhand, and striking with the open palm. They also permit the use of elbows, knees, and feet. In other words you can hit your opponent with everything you have got. There is no below-the-belt immunity; every part of the body is a legitimate target. For example the fighters will often lead with a quick kick to the head or stomach, then follow through with a knee jab to the groin and a series of haymakers to the head. If their arms become entwined, as they often do, they knee each other in the groin or the stomach. Only when a fighter is down is he free from attack. There seems to be little science. The boys simply go at each other hammer and tongs with caution thrown to the winds. Of course, they duck many blows and kicks, as these are clearly telegraphed beforehand, but a good many connect and the fight gets brutal and bloody.

In spite of the wild way of fighting the boxers were remarkably clean fighters according to their own rules. They obeyed the referee instantly and showed a fine spirit of sportsmanship in their conduct. The fans were rabid and were betting on every round in every fight. Apart from yelling and shouting, though, there was no sign of approval or disapproval in the form of applause or booing.

June 10, 1952

For the past few days I have pooled my resources with a Jewish fellow from New York and have been trying to see as much as possible as cheaply as possible. Yesterday morning we went to the Temple of the Reclining Buddha. The temple is still used and has a large number of priests living there, but it is badly in need of repair. The temple area must include about twenty-five buildings and covers about a quarter of a square mile. The main statue of the Buddha is enormous. It is lying on its side, resting its head on its right arm. The image is about one hundred and fifty feet long and about forty feet high. Except for the head and the feet, there is little detail, however, so it is impressive more in size than in beauty. We also went to the Royal Palace and the Temple of the Emerald Buddha. These are among the most beautiful structures in Bangkok. One cannot enter even the courtyard of the Palace without wearing a coat and tie. The Palace was really impressive but we were allowed to see only the coronation hall and the funeral hall, which were situated at opposite ends of the second courtyard. All of any actual living quarters as well as the official buildings were closed to us. Thailand may be a small country but she has a lot of pride. And although she treats tourists from America with respect and courtesy she refuses to overlook national customs. Before entering the Temple of the Emerald Buddha we removed our shoes. This temple is connected with the Royal Palace and is the official temple in which the King worships. The temple is impressive, but the actual Emerald Buddha is a little disappointing because it is small and placed high above a huge altar. It is one of the most sacred of the world's Buddhas, however. In another huge tower in the temple grounds is reputed to be a holy relic of the Lord Buddha himself.

Chapter 3

Although I enjoyed my few days in Bangkok, I am never content to stay long in a large urban area. I am still a small-town boy at heart and I like to get out of cities as soon as I can. Transportation was still poor in Thailand, and there were few places one could get to in any comfort. A long train journey seemed the most sensible trip, so I asked for a ticket to the end of the line.

"Chiengmai?"

"Is that the end of the railroad?"

"Yes, the end. The end."

My ticket was for a second-class sleeper. First-class sleepers, which were more expensive, entitled one to a special, insect-screened compartment. My ticket at that time did not entitle me to even a blanket.

The journey from Bangkok to Chiengmai took twenty-two hours. The first part took me through wide expanses of rice fields, broken here and there by clumps of palm trees or small wooded areas concealing a village. Often the only building visible among the trees was the pagoda of the village temple, glinting in the evening sun.

By seven o'clock it was too dark to see anything. Not until several years later was I able to mark where the scenery changed from flat rice lands to low scrub and, finally, mountainous jungle.

When I woke up the next morning we were slowly climbing the

mountains. The railroad was single track and it wound its way through and over the hills. Finally the terrain flattened out and we were in the Chiengmai plain—a flat, fairly well-wooded area broken up into truck gardens, plantations, and rice fields. The entire plain is surrounded by low mountains that range in color according to the light and time of day, from dark green to a hazy cigarette-smoke blue. The city itself is compacted within a few square miles, and it is dominated by the nearest mountain, Mt. Sutep. On top of the mountain at about twenty-five hundred feet, a temple glitters white and gold against the western sky. In 1952 Chiengmai was a slumbering provincial town with a glorious history, a reputation for pretty girls, a locally famous fruit cash crop (*lamyai*, sometimes called *longyen*) and very little else. Today it is a thriving, bustling city snaking out suburban tentacles in every direction, with a university, a modern airport, and all the accessories of a tourist trap.

And yet in spite of its overcrowded streets and modern bustle it has retained much of its old charm. The people are as courteous and friendly as before. A few miles out of Chiengmai, in any direction, and one is back in the old Thailand again, and one feels that it would take very little for the jungle and scrub to reclaim lost territories.

Fourteen years ago Chiengmai had still to be "discovered" and tourists were a rarity. The city lacked comfortable hotels and there were few if any amenities for a foreign visitor. I booked in at a room at the old Railway Terminus Hotel and waited for something to happen. I had heard that there were elephants in the area and hoped to see them.

The American Consul, whom I visited regarding my travel documents, was a most hospitable man. There happened to be a few Americans visiting the town on business and pleasure of one kind or another and we were all invited to a cocktail party. Here I met a colonel in the U.S. Army. He had the use of a jeep and offered to take me around with him on his tour of the area.

24

My diary records the events of the next few days, and as they mark the beginning of my real life in Thailand and of my stumbling attempt to find some useful work to do, I should like to quote fairly fully.

June 19, 1952

Yesterday morning the American colonel, another tourist, and I went off in search of some working elephants. The road soon got very bad in places and we had to drive through several small streams. Finally the road gave out completely. However, within less than a mile we came in sight of the elephants. They were actually a small crew of six elephants with one baby and they were working with about fifty men.

The operation was only a cleaning-up process. The river down which the logs had been floating was very shallow in places and the logs had jammed here and there along the sand bars. The crew was going down the river and pulling loose all the logs and generally tidying up. Often the heavy teakwood logs were deeply mired into the sand, and the elephants either pushed with their heads or trunks or pulled with the heavy chain harness they wore. They were able to free the logs with little noticeable effort, but sometimes they had to drag them for fifty yards or so before they would float freely again. Whenever a log was set free and continued floating down the river one or more of the workmen climbed aboard and tried to guide it downstream like a raft or boat. The men pushed off the sand bars with poles and maneuvered the logs quite expertly, but the logs seldom floated more than a hundred yards before they became stranded again and it was necessary for the elephants to go downriver and start pulling them out all over again.

The elephants seemed to move slowly and yet the river was cleaned out surprisingly fast. One phase of the operation surprised me as it was more complicated than I had gathered from books and movies. This was the way the drivers handled the elephants. I knew that the drivers moved their legs behind the elephants' ears to start, stop, and turn them but I had never seen or heard how they handled the stubborn whims of the animal. When the driver wanted the elephant to move, he raised his legs up and down, almost bouncing on the animal's head. When he stopped bouncing the elephant stopped moving. To turn the elephants the drivers prodded them on one side of the head or the other, but when an elephant refused to respond to these gentle commands the excitement began. Each driver carried with him a large knife, similar to a machete. When an elephant balked, the driver hit him on the head with the butt of the knife. If he continued to balk he cracked him with the back of the blade, and if he still persisted in being ornery the driver stabbed down with the knife and cut open the top of the elephant's head. During this battle of wits the elephant shook his head violently and tried to throw the driver and cried out with rage. The driver hung on to the harness belt with one hand and used the knife with the other and eventually managed to subdue the animal. These little disputes occurred quite frequently.

The baby elephant was quite a problem child. It had to accompany its mother everywhere or else neither the mother nor the baby would behave properly. The little brute was bad-tempered and butted or charged anyone who happened to annoy him. He was not really big enough to cause any damage but he worked himself into the most fierce temper and screamed with fury whenever someone pushed him away or hopped on his back. And of course whenever he screamed his mother stopped whatever she was doing until she could make sure that he was in no danger.

During the next two or three days I visited with the colonel a number of places in the Chiengmai Province and then on Friday, June 20, he suggested that we ought to visit the leper colony on the outskirts of Chiengmai city. I was not too anxious to go along,

26

as the idea of leprosy had always frightened me. But I had no good reason for turning down the invitation, so I went along. At that time there were about five hundred patients in the actual leprosy colony and another two thousand scattered among leprosy villages in the area. It is estimated that about 1 to 2½ per cent of the total Thai population of twenty-seven million people have leprosy. This means that approximately four hundred thousand or more people have leprosy or have had leprosy recently. The colony, which is named after its founder, Dr. McKean, is administered by the Presbyterian Mission in Thailand. Most of its funds come from the American Leprosy Mission, some from the Thai government and local charities.

I was pleasantly surprised by the layout of the colony. Apart from the usual hospital wards and dormitories, many cabins had been built so that families could live together. The colony was far from self-supporting, but the patients worked in the gardens, grew a certain amount of food, and kept chickens and ducks.

No amenities, however, could hide the horror of leprosy. I know it is fashionable in America nowadays to refer to leprosy as Hansen's disease and to minimize the misery and suffering it causes, but to my mind it is one of the most horrible afflictions a person can have. During my visit I saw men and women with nothing left of their hands and feet except rough, uneven stumps. The faces of many patients were badly deformed where the bridges of their noses had collapsed, and the ears of some were pendulous and puffy. In addition to the physical deformity the patients suffered mentally. They had been shunned by their society and cast out. They knew they were ugly and unwanted, and I thought I could detect in their eyes a loss of hope.

After my visit I returned to the hotel in a confused state of mind. On the one hand I was impressed and heartened by the apparently selfless work of the missionaries, but at the same hand I was depressed by the misery and ugliness I had seen. That night I lay in bed and wondered whether the visit to McKean Colony had any significance for me. Here I was at the end of the line in Thailand, a country I had not even originally intended visiting. I had been prevented from joining my friend Dr. Wong and had drifted into Thailand with no plans. Was it possible, I asked myself, that God had led me deliberately to Chiengmai? I did not know, but I realized that I could not leave Chiengmai without taking at least one more step along this new path.

I decided to visit the McKean Colony again the next day and see what, if anything, happened.

The director of the colony then was Dr. Richard S. Buker. When I called on him and told him a little of my story he took me on a longer tour of the colony and explained the background of his work, the problems, and what he hoped to achieve. He told me that no one has yet proved what causes leprosy, and that the scientists will say no more than that *mycobacterium leprae* is probably the cause of the disease. The disease can be transmitted to other people from a nasal discharge, but not from the breath as such diseases as colds and influenza are. It can be transmitted in the mucus and serum to a cut on the skin, but there is no evidence to suggest that it can be picked up from cups and saucers or anything else associated with eating, drinking, or going to the bathroom. Some doctors, Dr. Buker told me, think that leprosy can be picked up by the feet, and there is some evidence to support this theory: the disease is endemic in hot countries where people walk barefoot, and it tends to be located in some areas more than in others. But this is only a theory. It can be argued that one finds "pockets" of the disease because of certain irregularities in the diet, or simply because a person suffering from leprosy—for example, a schoolteacher—may come into contact with many people in a certain area.

There are two kinds of leprosy: the lepromatous type and the tuberculoid or neural type. Both can be caused by the same baccilus and it is possible for a patient to suffer from a combination of both types. The lepromatous type is very infectious and generally attacks the skin, which becomes red and puffy in patches. The patient's ears become enlarged and his nose caves in. Although it looks bad it is rarely if ever crippling, provided that the patient is given drugs to arrest the course of the disease.

The tuberculoid type appears first as a spot on the skin with a distinct border around it. It involves the nerves and can result in crippling of the feet and hands and facial paralysis, which in turn may cause blindness as the patient cannot control the muscles of his eyelids and the eyes may become infected from dirt and dust. As the nerves of the extremities become affected they cease to register pain, and patients can easily burn or bruise themselves seriously without knowing it. Also, as the nerve endings no longer register any feeling, fingers and toes tend to wither away and there are muscular contractions causing the "claw hand" and "drop foot" which are so typical of the disease. At this stage, surgery is often necessary to cut away useless parts of the hands and feet. Dr. Buker explained that because leprosy patients cannot feel anything in the affected parts it is not usually necessary to use any kind of anesthetic for surgical repair. He also told me that the presence of anesthetic areas is a useful indication in the diagnosis of leprosy.

All this information and much more Dr. Buker passed on to me as we walked about the colony. From time to time he would stop walking and refer me to a particular patient as an example of what he was saying.

When I asked whether leprosy could be cured, Dr. Buker explained that "cured" was the wrong word. He preferred to use the word "arrested." An arrested case is one in which smears taken will be negative of *mycobacterium leprae*. There are also "burnt-out" cases, patients in whom the disease has burnt itself out, in the sense of a forest fire that has died out and will not catch again because there is nothing left to burn. But whereas an arrested case may show no signs of the disease and may never have a recurrence, a burnt-out case is usually permanently crippled and deformed. Few of the afflicted die from leprosy. When leprosy patients do die it is nearly always from secondary complications, such as pneumonia or infections. With early diagnosis and treatment, however, much can be done to arrest cases before they become too advanced. [Dr. Buker's complete "Analysis of Leprosy Control Methods" is included as an appendix at the end of this book.]

At the end of our walk we returned to Dr. Buker's house in the colony and he asked me what I wanted to do with myself. I said I did not know, and so he suggested that I might like to stay on at the colony for a couple of months. He said that while I thought about my future I could be learning about the diagnosis and treatment of leprosy and making myself generally useful. Within a few days, he told me, there would be a vacant room for me, and I could live in the colony and eat with him and his wife.

Although I was still not attracted to this kind of work—I was not, after all, a doctor nor even had training in nursing—I knew I could not refuse. A door had been opened for me, and after my aimless wandering there was only one thing I could in all honesty do, walk through it, and hope that if there was work for me I should be capable of doing it.

I accepted Dr. Buker's invitation and moved out of the hotel to live with a missionary family for a few days until my room was ready.

July 3, 1952

This morning I went with Dr. Buker on a checkup visit to three of his downriver leprosy villages. The villages are nothing more than clusters of native huts just like any other little village. The only difference is that every one of these has a small church. Not readily discernible, the churches are built and look like all the other native leaf-roofed huts.

Dr. Buker told me that about half of the people who contract leprosy have such mild cases that they get well again without medication and possibly without ever knowing that they have had the disease. Of the other half who need treatment about 75 per cent get well or at least have the growth of the disease arrested with hardly any noticeable effects if they have been treated in time. But the other 25 per cent or so suffer terribly. This morning I had a close, careful look at some of the worst cases. Their faces are puffed up and their noses are caved in so that they are almost flat with the face. The hands and feet are just stumps and look as if they have been cut off in an accident. Often the whole body is covered with scabs and open sores. How these extreme cases are able to feed and dress themselves is a mystery to me. Not only are the fingers and often the hands gone, but the stumps that are left sometimes give much pain. To add to their woes, they usually become afflicted with other diseases too. When they have leprosy in an acute stage their strength is reduced and their appetite impaired and their resistance is lowered accordingly.

This morning one poor man came for treatment and presented what I think is the most miserable appearance I have ever seen. He had lost all his fingers and most of both feet and his completely tattooed body was covered with sores. Perhaps the worst thing about him was the pained and sick expression on his face. He also had a stoppage of the bowels, apparently caused by an internal growth, and according to Dr. Buker he was showing the symptoms of cancer. The man must have been in extreme misery all the time and yet he did exactly what he was told without uttering any complaints. I wonder if I shall have the stomach for this work. I used to think I was fairly tough, but this kind of thing is almost too much for me.

July 5, 1952

This is my second night at the leprosy colony and I think I shall settle in fairly well. Dr. Buker and his wife are easy to get along with. They live frugally, making no pretenses to grandeur. I am made to feel part of the family. It is this kind of hospitality that makes me feel I want to do my share, so that I can feel completely at home with them.

Dr. Buker gave me a copy of the leprosy textbook we shall use in our studies, and he also gave me a preliminary lesson and study plan. This course is going to be far more comprehensive and difficult than I supposed. It is also going to be far more gruesome. It seems that I arrived here at exactly the right time. I shall be one of seven students in the course who are coming to Chiengmai from all over Thailand to study leprosy under Dr. Buker, who is, I am told, something of a world authority.

July 6, 1952

This morning Dr. Buker had to perform an emergency appendectomy on the son of the watchman. The surgery was done here in the leprosy hospital operating room and I had the privilege of observing it. This was the first operation I had ever seen performed and it really impressed me. I was astounded by the way Dr. Buker reached down into the incision with both hands and with instruments until he could pull the appendix outside of the body to do the cutting. Later when I thought about it, it seemed that everything had been done the only practical way, and yet as I watched it being done I was surprised. It is amazing how completely uninformed I have been about surgery and medicine. My experiences here are giving me a much greater respect for the training of a doctor. As I was watching the operation, several times my stomach felt a little peculiar. I suppose the sight of blood was almost more than I could stand. I did not get sick but I felt uneasy.

Although I had the closest and best seat at the operation I was not the only spectator. Half of the inhabitants of the colony seemed to be crowded outside looking in through the windows. It was quite funny to see them hanging from precarious positions to watch the show. You would think that people afflicted as they are would be tired of doctors and surgery, but no, they seemed to be even more interested than most people.

The thing that impressed me most of all was the prayer just before the incision was made. The patient had been given a spinal injection and all the towels and covers were in place. The instruments were laid out and the final check made. Then, as Dr. Buker picked up the knife, the entire group stopped and bowed their heads and the nurse led a prayer in Thai. The group consisted of Dr. Buker and his Thai assistant; Mrs. Buker, who is a registered nurse; a Thai nurse; and three young Thai patients who have been trained to help around the hospital.

July 9, 1952

I started the leprosy training in earnest yesterday and it seems as if I am going to be hard pressed to find time to keep up my entries in this diary. Time really flies when you are doing something interesting.

So far I have cut or trimmed several patients' feet. When the foot ulcerates, the treatment is to cut off all the dry dead flesh around the ulcer and then clean out the ulcerations. These ulcers often go right to the bone and they smell bad. It seems strange to take a knife and a pair of forceps and cut off pieces of a person's foot. The only thing that keeps me from passing out is my intense interest. We cut off flesh until it begins to bleed, and yet the patient does not feel any pain because of the anesthesia caused by the disease. Besides trimming feet, we have also done some injecting of arm nerves to relieve pain in the patients' hands.

This disease scares the wits out of me now that I am seeing it up close. I do not know why I do not take off to some place as far away from a leprosy area as I can get.

33

July 13, 1952

The time has been flying! Every morning we are busy, first with
a lecture and then with cutting and trimming or giving shots. In
the afternoon we spend the time practicing charting and diagnos-
ing patients, and then finish the afternoon with golf or badmin-
ton. By the time we have cleaned up and finished supper we are
about ready for bed. It seems I have no time to keep up my diary.

Last night we attended a classical play that the patients put on
in their theater. At one time a member of the royal theater group
was a patient in the colony. She and another lady with theater
experience encouraged the writing and direction of these plays
and they are still performed once a month.

Considering the resources these lepers have to work with, they
put on a splendid production. Some of the costumes and plots
were rather crude but they seemed entirely adequate to their purpose. The play was a typical Thai drama, similar to the one I saw
in Bangkok. Most of the players did not have bad cases of leprosy,
but a few with either a drop or stump foot took part. It was really
inspiring to see the enjoyment that everyone got out of performing this play. It was such a contrast to the type of life that everyone thinks a leper must of necessity live. There is no doubt that
the lives of these people are filled with suffering and pain and
misery. But it is equally obvious that under the type of system
Dr. Buker is trying to develop the leprosy patients will also have
opportunities to laugh and play and feel important in various types
of work in the colony.

This morning we went to a church service conducted by the
patients. A large majority of the lepers become Christians and
therefore the church is very active. Here they choose their own
pastor and elect their own officers and attend to all other affairs
without any outside interference.

34

The extreme interest of the patients in the service and the intent and eager look on their leprosy-swollen faces was as inspiring a sight as can be imagined.

The children in the colony are nearly always singing wherever they are. And the only tunes you hear are the familiar strains of often-sung hymns.

July 15, 1952

We had a rest this afternoon so I have a chance to catch up with my diary again. During these last two days we have been mainly concerned with giving intradermal injections of hydnocarpus oil. Not only is this hard work for us but it hurts the patient considerably. The entire process is therefore rather a strain, since the heavy oil is not easily forced between the layers of skin. These injections used to be the only method of treatment. It must have been trying for both patients and doctor. I am certainly glad that new drugs given in the form of pills and tablets have almost eliminated this painful procedure. Hydnocarpus oil is now given only as supplemental treatment in those cases in which it has beneficial results on individual muscles and localized skin areas.

Today we began real surgery on infected bones of feet and hands. There are simply not enough qualified surgeons available in rural areas, and so if the leprosy victims are to be cared for it falls upon trainees like us to do the job. Hopefully this shortage may be met in future years. My turn has not come yet to operate so I only observed today. The patients walked in and lay down on the operating table. Each patient had a part of a hand or foot removed and then walked out of the operating room again. It was almost unbelievable. Of course, the absence of sensitivity explained why the patients had infections in the first place. They had not been aware that they had bruised or burnt themselves. Therefore they were not treated and infection had set in.

Tomorrow and Thursday we shall visit some of the outlying villages.

Yesterday I received a letter from Dr. Wong. He wants to study in America but he needs a hospital acceptance before he can get a passport. If my family cannot get an acceptance for him, I think I shall have to go home soon and obtain it for him myself. I expect I shall have learned enough here by then anyway.

July 19, 1952

On Wednesday we went by jeep to Chomtong, a town about forty-five miles southwest of here, and visited three leprosy villages in that area. On Thursday we went by train to Lampang, where we spent the night and visited two more villages. We returned home by train Friday evening. Visiting these villages is always interesting for me not only because of the countryside but because of the people and their problems. Dr. Buker is trying to help them be self-supporting, so he buys them pigs and cows to get them started. Much of the discussion, therefore, is about pig transactions and how long it will be before the village can be free of its debts. Lepers have been used to charity and isolation from others for so long that they are sometimes slow to try to become self-supporting again. They have got used to the idea of having something for nothing even though the something is meager.

The real purpose behind leprosy work here seems to be Christian missionary work, and naturally much is said concerning religious progress. Most of the leprosy patients appear to be sincere in wanting to become Christians but they are badly in need of proper instruction. Every village except one has a church and an active congregation, but there are many problems. The pastors the patients elect are often lacking in training. Evangelists are sent to each village occasionally but they are not all well informed

36

either. As the evangelists are lepers themselves, they are not usually welcomed by the larger established churches. The most common problem seems to be a shortage of charity and forgiveness. If a person misbehaves the congregation usually kicks him out of the church. They sometimes also stop giving him his leprosy medicine. I am not at all happy about finding this kind of behavior in so-called Christian communities and neither is Dr. Buker. But it is impossible for me and difficult for Dr. Buker to interfere in this aspect of the leprosy program.

Another purpose of our visit was to examine any person suffering from other illness and to treat him. There is a lot of malaria and typhoid among the villagers.

Dr. Buker has a supply of old eyeglasses that have been donated by people in America. Most of them are not in very good condition but they bring a lot of happiness. Patients whose eyes are getting bad try on various glasses until they find a pair they think might help them. It is pathetic and yet funny to watch a person discover a pair that suits him. His swollen and broken features break into a broad grin. For many long minutes he sits and studies his stumps of hands at various distances, glowing with happiness at his improved vision.

I think often the tendency is to look at a leper as a case or a number and to work mechanically on his treatment. But if you take time to study the patients you soon realize they are people with feelings like anyone else. They become vitally interesting personalities who tear at your heart when you realize the pain and discouragements they have suffered. When you look at a broken shell of a person and realize that he is beyond physical aid it almost makes you cry, especially if he looks at you with trusting eyes expecting a miraculous cure.

The women leprosy patients are just as proud as women anywhere, and they primp to the best of their abilities when they are to be treated or inspected. Often their hands are so crippled that it is extremely painful for them to use them, and yet they will immediately change clothes and pretty up their hair as best they can if we drive unexpectedly into the village.

This morning I performed my first surgery involving bone cutting and amputation. I operated on a man with a badly infected and swollen foot that had been discharging pus. Dr. Buker gave continuous instructions, of course, but he made me do all the work. I cut open the heel of the foot to allow it to drain better and then scraped off some of the bone. Then I removed a toe and cleaned up the front part of the foot. After I had removed the toe I stitched up the wound. I no longer feel hollow in my stomach when I see open flesh with the blood pouring out, and I feel confident now that when I have completed my study here I shall be able to help Dr. Wong if we can ever get together again.

July 25, 1952

This morning we completed the last stage of our leprosy training. The other students will be moving out tomorrow to their respective places in the mission field, but I have decided to stay on here and assist Dr. Buker for as long as he wants me.

This past week we have operated more and checked patients whom we have previously treated.

Yesterday we visited two more villages north of here about fifty and a hundred miles away respectively. This trip was by far the most beautiful and most interesting I have yet made. We left early in the morning by jeep. After about an hour's drive we stopped at Mae Tang, where I applied for another extension of stay for my visa. While waiting there for the immigration man to come, we had a chance to look around. Down by the river there were three elephants hauling logs into the river so that the logs could be tied into rafts and floated downstream during high water.

In the village the natives had a bear they had captured. It was the oddest-looking bear I have ever seen. He was black with a white chest and stomach and had little round ears like a Teddy bear. He seemed to be halfway between a panda and the usual kind of black bear.

After we left Mae Tang we climbed into the mountains and jungle regions. It reminded me of the movie settings of Tarzan pictures. [Oddly enough a movie entitled *Tarzan's Three Challenges* was filmed in this locality in 1963.] The road wound around, up and over in a way that was hard on the car and the driver but ideal for sightseeing. Every so often we passed logging stations where elephants were pulling logs into position to be loaded onto huge trucks and carried to the river a few miles away. I do not think I shall ever tire of looking at elephants. At one place we only just missed running over a king cobra that slithered across the road ahead of us.

We visited the first village in the morning and ate our dinner in a small native restaurant nearby. While we were eating, a large group of hill tribespeople gathered around to watch us. These tribespeople are fascinating. Each tribe was dressed differently, but they all chewed betel nut and had red mouths and black teeth. They wore turbans and leggings and strangely designed shirts and shorts. These tribespeople raise opium. Their homes are a half day's walk into the mountains and they come into the villages only to buy rice.

To get to the last village we had to leave the main road and drive three miles into the jungle. The road was cut only for ox-carts and pedestrians, so occasionally we had to dig up tree stumps or drive around fallen trees or through buffalo wallows, and the vegetation was too thick to see much. The jeep finally made it in low-ratio four-wheel drive.

The villages themselves were similar to the others that I had seen. The patients were checked and very sick people were treated.

39

Eyeglasses were given to those who asked for them and a small supply of medicines was left.

We arrived home thoroughly tired.

July 27, 1952

The other members of the leprosy class have all left for their various stations, and the house is quiet and empty.

Tomorrow I start learning my duties as an assistant with the work here. Much of my time, of course, will have to be spent in studying the Thai language. I am determined to stay here only if I can prove of use to Dr. Buker. It seems to me as if he has too much dead wood around already.

Yesterday we went up the mountain to look over a possible site for a mission resthouse. I was surprised by how much difference two thousand feet made in the temperature. It was gorgeous on top of the mountain.

On the way down we were stopped by a heavily armed group of police who were checking for an opium runner who was reportedly coming through with a large shipment of opium. We had already met this opium dealer on the road, so we knew that he was still up the mountain. Usually smugglers buy off the local officials so that nothing is ever heard about their dealings. But occasionally a small official is either overlooked or he pulls a double cross and a shipment is confiscated. A month or so ago an opium runner was shot and killed with a "ton" of opium in his car. Apparently the right person was not bought off yesterday, which would explain why the police were there. Opium is the only source of income for most of the hill tribespeople and so it is naturally difficult to keep them from growing it. Unless an equally lucrative crop is shown to them as a substitute I am afraid the raising of opium will continue as a matter of economic necessity here. And as long as it is raised there will always be people to smuggle and smoke it.

August 9, 1952

Two weeks have passed since my last entry in this book but I have been too busy to write up my experiences. I am afraid that after two weeks of language study I am not encouraged. I have, I suppose, made some progress but when I compare what I know with what I still have to learn I am tempted to call the whole idea off. Not only do I have to learn to speak and understand what I hear, but I have to learn a new kind of alphabet and to read and write at the same time. Fortunately my duties are kept light. I am in charge of the wood carving and I am trying to establish a profitable business for the colony. The idea is to give the carvers an incentive to work faster by paying them by piece work. Previously they received nothing for their work except the rice, housing, and medicine which were given to all the patients whether they worked or not. Now we are going to pay a special bonus of about one dollar for each set of carved bookends. This week the seven men finished twelve sets so maybe this incentive is what they needed. I hope I can build up this business and earn a few dollars for the colony, because the budget does not go very far.

I have also been bringing up to date all the patients' records. I have been making charts and taking pictures of all the new patients.

By the end of the first week in August I had been living and working in the colony for just over a month. Dr. Buker and his wife had already become a second family to me. Dr. Buker himself is a remarkably dynamic personality. He originally came to the Far East to work in Burma with his twin brother, an ordained minister in the Baptist Church, and did in fact work with a mission to the Shan States in Northern Burma until the outbreak of World War II. During the war, when Burma was occupied by the

Japanese, Dr. Buker worked in South America; then after the defeat of the Japanese he tried to return to his work in Burma. But the political situation had changed, as had the Burmese policy toward missionaries, and the continuation of his work in Burma became impossible. However, at that time the McKean Colony in Chiengmai, which had become rather run-down during the war, needed a new driving force to reorganize it. The American Leprosy Mission—a purely fund-raising organization with no field workers—suggested to the Presbyterian Mission that Dr. Buker, Baptist though he was, might be the best man to get the McKean Colony on its feet again.

Dr. Buker's ideas have been criticized in some quarters recently but I feel he has a very real understanding of the problems. He wants the McKean Colony to be as self-supporting as possible. When I first worked at McKean it needed a yearly budget of $35,000. Dr. Buker felt that the money should not be spent solely for the benefit of the colony but that it should be spread as widely as possible. I think he felt that it was wrong to try to featherbed one small group of leprosy patients when outside the colony there were hundreds of thousands of patients receiving practically no help. His policy was to take patients into the colony for as brief a time as possible, give them the necessary treatment and surgery, and then discharge them. It would have been so easy to establish McKean as a home for idle lepers, but this would have been bad for the patients themselves and bad for leprosy work in general. If there is only a limited amount of money available it has to be spread as widely, albeit thinly, as possible. At least this was Dr. Buker's policy and as my own work developed I adopted it as my own.

Apart from my admiration for Dr. and Mrs. Buker, the thing that was to decide the course of my life was my friendship with a young Thai worker in the McKean Colony. Surin, who was an arrested case of leprosy, worked as an assistant to Dr. Buker. Surin was my age and he had come to the colony with a slight infection which had been successfully arrested. His family was fairly well off and he had had a good education. Dr. Buker, who was a man never to miss an opportunity, had realized how valuable a man like Surin would be to the colony, and had persuaded him to stay on as staff.

My friendship with Surin did not begin until after the course. Then, when I had more free time, I started English classes for the Thai staff—most of whom, like Surin, were arrested cases of leprosy. In addition to Surin, there was Twee, who was the colony schoolteacher; Wichit and Mungkorn, assistants in the clinic; and Boonkrong, the bookkeeper-*cum*-business manager. But for me, Surin stood out from the others. Not only was his English already fairly good, which made it easier for us to communicate, but he was interested in politics and political science, and his conversation and ideas seemed to have more depth than those of the others. He asked me intelligent questions about America and queried the rightness of many aspects of our way of life.

When he had first arrived at the colony Surin had been rather anti-American. He had felt that any Americans who shut themselves away in some remote corner of Thailand could not be much good. If they were good, he had argued, why were they not holding down good jobs in America? He had also been exposed to a great deal of anti-American propaganda and resented everything America was doing in the Far East. But Dr. Buker had taken him in hand and, realizing that Surin was an extremely capable young man, had given him as complete a medical education as circumstances allowed. He had become a protégé of the Bukers, and their faith in him had been justified. By the time I arrived at McKean, Surin had already accepted the Christian faith and was working as Dr. Buker's chief assistant in the clinic.

I shall never forget the account he gave of his first night in the colony. It was a chilly night. He had been issued blankets but even though they were clean and smelled of moth balls it was also obvious that they had been used. Did this place expect him to

43

sleep under blankets previously used by a leper? He would rather freeze and he nearly did before his shivering fingers pulled up the blankets to ward off the damp penetrating fog of the early morning. Then his roommate began stumbling around in the dark and wasted long minutes trying to strike a match to light a fire. Surin angrily snatched the match away. When he lit it he realized the poor fellow had been trying to ignite the wrong end. It was dark and his fingers simply couldn't feel which end of the match stick held the head. Surin couldn't help wondering what kind of a place he was getting into.

My friendship with Surin counts as a real turning point in my life. He was my only friend of my own age and had it not been for him I doubt whether I would ever have started an independent leprosy program on my own. But many things were to happen before Surin and I even thought of starting a rehabilitation village.

My diary at this time is rather disjointed. I was too busy and, I think, too happy to spend much time writing down the events of each day. However, there were a number of incidents that seemed important to me at the time, and I have recorded them briefly in the diary.

August 16, 1952

The time flies by! Another week has gone and I am as poor in the language as ever. However, we are making some progress with the wood carving, even though much of the teakwood has cracks in it. These cracks are caused by bad curing and drying, and they spoil the wood for carving. In addition to our difficulties in finding good wood we have a hard time finding enough good bone for the tusks of the elephants we are carving. [Later we found a splendid source of bone in an unlicensed buffalo slaughterhouse. The owners were only too delighted to get rid of incriminating bones.] Despite the wood shortage the carvers have finished fifteen pairs of bookends this week. I think they could have done even more but there seems to be a quarrel developing between two groups of carvers. I do not know what it is all about yet but I hope it does not develop into anything serious.

This morning I watched Dr. Buker remove a bladder stone from a two-year-old baby. How a child so young could develop a stone like this is more than we can figure out. The stone is about one inch long and half an inch thick. I helped to hold the child while ether was given, and generally did the work of an operating-room technician. I was surprised at how conditioned I have become to the sight of blood. The worst part of the whole business today was prior to giving the child the anesthetic. The baby was too young to understand what was going on and wailed and sobbed when we held him down on the table. His little heart pounded away and I felt very sorry for him, but there was nothing either of us could do to calm him down.

After the operation we went to the crematorium and attended the cremation of a man who died here last night. The man had no family or friends who cared for him and there were no mourners. As he was a non-Christian, the service for him was very brief. The Christian pastor, a leprosy patient, and the other Christians in the colony waste very little time or words on any non-Christian who dies. At times like this my mind begins to question some of the workings of Christianity in this colony.

September 7, 1952

I am enjoying an ideal existence. Although we seem to be fairly safe inside the McKean Colony, there is enough action and intrigue going on in the surrounding countryside to supply a library of material for writers of adventure stories. Only last night, for example, I was taken from my peaceful world and exposed to the brutal world outside. The recent floods have caused many teak

logs to break loose and float down the river. Because of the location of our colony by the side of the river, the patients have been capturing these runaway logs and holding them for the reward paid by the teak lumber companies. This is a perfectly legitimate thing to do. However, it has not been as easy as it sounds. Stealing teak logs has become a large and profitable business here in the north and naturally enough the local criminals are determined to cash in on it. They do not approve of our leprosy patients receiving the rewards. A few days ago we heard that our patients had been forced at gunpoint to release the logs they had caught. Around nine o'clock last night we were alarmed by several patients who informed us that about ten armed thieves were actually in the colony again stealing the logs that had been caught. Dr. Buker grabbed his shotgun and I took his .22 rifle and we rushed over to the other side of the island. We may have hurried the thieves a little, but we were too late to catch them as they had already set loose five logs and gone. We could hear noises from across and down the river but as we had no boat we could not investigate further. We still have ten logs left here, so I hope that if the thieves come again we shall have a better chance of catching them.

This teak stealing seems to be getting out of hand. In Chiengmai at this moment there are logs and rafts linked together in caravan style prepared for a dash down the river. There are fifteen houses on the rafts, each with a gun mounting. The total crew numbers about seventy-five men, and yet they are not the least confident about being able to run through the thieves' blockade farther down the river.

Opium smuggling also seems to be on the increase. The police put up surprise road blocks in an attempt to stop opium traffic, but in some places the opium smugglers are too strong for the police. The police raided a village north of here several weeks ago but they were badly shot up. They have not even been able to recover their dead and wounded, because every truckload of police that goes into the jungle gets shot up by the smugglers.

One village nearby has had twelve murders in two months as a result of opium dealings and double crossings. Three headless corpses were recovered floating down the river the other day. It is very surprising what a peaceful existence I am able to live in the midst of all this excitement.

Last Friday I helped Mrs. Buker distribute donated clothing to the leprosy women. In an effort to ensure fair distribution, each woman took a number and was then given the article of clothing corresponding to the number. The women looked pathetic with their club feet, deformed hands, and badly disfigured faces. And yet they reminded me of almost any group of ladies at a rummage sale. They gossiped and shouted and pushed one another to get to the front. Our method of distribution produced some amusing results.

It seemed that the oldest and most disfigured women drew numbers providing them with chic new strapless bathing suits or summer frocks while the young belles of the colony received matronly dresses or thick underwear. What a variety of exchanges and transactions ensued! Although most of the stuff was junk I think everyone was satisfied when the distribution was finally over. Of course, a person who has nothing to start with is not too difficult to satisfy.

September 8, 1952

Today I fulfilled one of my lifelong ambitions. I rode on an elephant. We have been having such a time trying to keep the logs which have floated down the river that the timber company finally sent two elephants to pull them out of the river and get them ready to be hauled away by truck. The elephants and their drivers arrived last evening, and the beasts were hobbled and left on the island in front of our house.

This morning they went to work and I was given the privilege of riding the biggest one. I was as happy as a small child, and I think everyone else was happy to see me so happy. The elephant I rode was a big tusker, standing about eleven or twelve feet high, but he seemed much higher than that when I got on top of him. There was no saddle of any kind but I was able to hang on to the harness. And I had to hang on for dear life! When the elephant knelt to push or lunged forward to pull I needed all my strength to stay on. I rode around for about an hour. We went shoulder deep into the water to retrieve logs, and it was like sitting on a moving island. We pulled logs across fields and down roads and hauled them out of the mud. When the elephant was walking down the road, we moved in a swaying jolting rhythm that was not too uncomfortable although I am told that many people get "seasick" on an elephant.

September 21, 1952

It rains and rains and rains. I have been living a fairly routine existence, studying the Thai language and charting the patients. The only difference is that now nearly everything is flooded and I have to wade through water to get anywhere.

It seems that this part of the world has been having an unusual number of typhoons this year. In Chiengmai we do not get the wind but we do get the rains that they bring. Since all the rivers and streams drain from the mountains all about us, it does not take long before they are raging torrents and everything is flooded. Many times the road to town has been covered by two or more feet of water and we have barely been able to get through. Yesterday I thought I would never make it. I had to drive a couple of the assistants to an agricultural school about fifteen miles north where we were promised some turkeys. In some places the road was flooded for several hundred yards with one to three feet of swirling raging water. It was hard enough trying to guess where the road was and where the ditches were, but the strong current made it worse. A couple of times we were tossed sideways and I thought we would be swept away but eventually we got through and collected the turkeys. Then I had the pleasure of driving all the way home again.

I have never seen people take a flood as calmly as the Thai people do. A few people are always drowned and possessions are lost but no one shows any emotions. Though most of the houses are built on stilts some of them get flooded anyway and most of the Chiengmai business area, which is not built on stilts, is flooded during the rainy season. It is funny to see people sitting at a restaurant table, knee deep in water, eating their meal as if nothing were the slightest bit unusual. The storekeepers prop up their goods on boxes and boards and continue as if nothing has happened. In some houses the children can be seen splashing around the sitting room having a great time. It is quite a different atmosphere from that I saw in the flooded areas of Omaha when I passed through there last April.

Nearly every week we are invited to a wedding among the patients. Contrary to what one might expect, these are fairly normal weddings. As many people come to the colony at the first signs of leprosy, they often do not develop any of the noticeable effects. Some of the girls are very attractive indeed, and in their wedding dresses they look stunning.

October 11, 1952

A few days ago I had to stop at the Immigration Office in Mae Tang to apply for an extension of my visa. I was told that the extension could not be given to me in Mae Tang but that I would have to go to the Head Immigration Office in Bangkok. Since I want very much to spend a Christmas at the colony I went to Bangkok to get the extension. I received an extension until January with no trouble and on the way back from Bangkok visited the Phra Pa Daeng Leprosy Colony. This is the largest government leprosy colony and although it is geographically near Bangkok it is very isolated. To get there we had to take a bus, then a small river launch, then walk a mile, and then take another boat. The colony depressed me with its dirt, drabness, and lack of spirit. The grass was uncut and the walks in bad repair. The people seemed to be completely without hope or spirit, their eyes were dull, and they wandered aimlessly about. Although the colony is not escape-proof, there are fences and guards keeping a strict watch over the inmates. From reports I have heard, the food and treatment are inadequate. Such depressing restrictive surroundings seem to destroy most of what is human in a person. It is not surprising that our Chiengmai colony is full of runaways from the Phra Pa Daeng Colony.

Although I am not an expert on leprosy colonies I do believe that this type of colony is typical of the places that for years have been the only havens for leprosy patients. I know there are financial and other problems involved in providing places for lepers, but I cannot accept the idea that the Phra Pa Daeng type of colony is the right answer. Neither is the McKean Colony, better though it is than Phra Pa Daeng. There must be a way of helping these people to live more normal and less institutionalized lives.

October 31, 1952

Dr. Buker has gone away for two weeks on a trip to Eastern Thailand and so I have been left in charge. Nothing too difficult has happened for me, however, and the patients manage to run everything very well themselves. They are most capable and could easily lead normal lives in a village given an initial push and a little financial assistance.

The only unusual incident occurred when a patient went mad

from side effects of the DDS treatment. This patient is normal most of the time, but when he goes off he struts about thinking that he is a king and goes through all sorts of weird dances and rituals. He preaches against foreigners and Christianity, stamps on the floor, screams, wails, and puts on a mighty performance. It is most distressing to see a man go out of his mind like this in front of you and be unable to do much about it. To calm him down we have tried injecting morphine and sometimes he snaps out of his fits fairly soon, but I am quite sure that we can expect repeated relapses. There is another mental case also. This poor man has been in the colony for some time now but he is quite harmless and appears to be happy although completely insane.

In spite of these unfortunate side effects, DDS, (diamino-diphenyl sulfone) is a boon to the treatment of leprosy. The drug does not actually kill the bacillus but in most cases it builds up a tissue resistance so that the bacillus is forced to retreat and lie dormant. This is the reason that leprosy cases are referred to as being arrested, and not cured, cases.

A very toxic drug, DDS must be handled with respect. It is virtually tasteless and will not cause nausea and therefore has become a rather favorite means of suicide for discouraged patients. I vividly remember several frantic occasions when we pumped out poisoned stomachs—not always successfully, alas.

Years later in our Trinity Village we experienced a most sorrowful tragedy. A two-year-old baby who was the darling of the village picked up some of his parents' DDS pills and ate them. Dr. Wong did all he could but the poor little fellow couldn't overcome the damage to his kidneys and died, leaving our village in tears.

During the last two weeks I have been trying to start a choir. The Thai have developed a kind of nasal whining style of singing. It defies description and is practically the opposite of what is required in the Western style of choral singing. As I have little musical talent, my attempts to train a Thai choir are causing considerable amusement.

It is very rewarding to be accepted by some of the people here and to be appreciated. At the same time it is disheartening to see that a large group of the patients resent any help of any kind from foreigners. They have an unreasonable but genuine hatred of foreigners and mission work. They resent any rules restricting their freedom and cry out loud and long at how unjust everyone is to them. They condemn our "capitalism" and also our ideas of charity, and yet the complainers are always the first ones to get in line for anything free. I suppose people are the same the world over: instead of being appreciative for what they get, they condemn because they have not received more. However, I believe that generally speaking, leprosy patients are far more appreciative than others, as they have usually suffered so much more despair and discouragement.

December 4, 1952

Today I visited an opium parlor in the city and found it quite unlike what I had expected. The place was licensed by the government and operated under government supervision. [Selling opium is now illegal in Thailand and the law is strictly enforced.] To reach it we went down a narrow alley and then turned into what appeared to be a bicycle shop. Behind the rows of bicycles at the back of the shop there were rows of berths for the opium smokers to lie in. A customer received his pipe at the counter by the door and then picked out a comfortable-looking berth. The beds were actually long boards; each was equipped with a pillow and a candle lamp. Opium was delivered to the customer as he asked for it, and it looked like syrup or hardened sap from a tree. The opium smoker held it over the candle lamp until it became soft. Then with a small pin he formed a small ball of it, put it in the compartment of the pipe, and held it over the candle lamp. As it gradually melted, the opium gave off fumes which the smoker inhaled.

The smokers lay quietly in their stalls as they smoked their opium and dreamed. The place was peaceful and orderly. It was quite different from the kind of opium den that I had seen in movies and read about in sensational magazines.

December 21, 1952

Dr. Buker has bought a film projector for the colony and I have been teaching the staff how to operate it. We have had three nights of movies so far. One of the movies was a story about leprosy that had been made a few years ago to solicit donations in America. It was a real tearjerker, but the patients thought it the funniest thing they had seen in years. During the scenes in which poor crippled lepers hobbled along, the patients roared with laughter. This seems to be typical of their attitude. They have overcome their own period of self-pity and are now able to joke and mock one another about crippled hands or feet. I suppose their suffering must be less severe now that they can laugh about it outwardly.

December 29, 1952

Well, I have spent my Christmas at the McKean Colony and what a wonderful Christmas it has been. The leprosy patients decorated the entire colony with paper flowers and streamers. They also set up their own small fair ground, with food stalls and places to play games in. On Tuesday, December 23, we gave a party for the leprosy children and distributed a few gifts. On Wednesday we gave a party for the well children (nonleprous children of leprosy patients) and then on Christmas Day we distributed gifts to the adult leprosy patients. On Wednesday evening we performed our concert and pageant and there was a short religious play given by the leprosy school.

Christmas Day began for me at the Bukers' Christmas tree

where we opened our presents. Then there was a church service followed by the distribution of presents to the patients, the leprosy-colony Christmas dinner, games and boxing, and, in the evening, a play.

On Friday we had more games and boxing and general celebrations which were concluded with a night parade of candlelit paper floats which the patients carried on poles over their shoulders. The parade stopped every now and then and the patients performed some Thai dances.

On Saturday we drove up to Fang and distributed blankets and leftovers at the two leper villages there. The trip over the mountains and through the jungle was as beautiful as ever. This time, however, we saw only two elephants and no game except birds.

This week has been completely satisfying except I was sickened by the trash sent out here by church people in America. I cannot understand how supposedly Christian people can unload all their worthless junk on Christian charities and feel decent about it. What good are rags of clothing and broken toys to these people? I wish that every person who gave such things had to present them personally to the leprosy patients and suffer the humiliation of offering such worthless gifts. If people would only buy some cheap but new and usable item instead of sending worthless worn-out things. The McKean Colony of course would not exist if it were not for Christian donations. But, when I look at the special Christmas donations—old clothing, broken toys and used Christmas cards—and compare them with the Buddhist donations, I am bitterly ashamed. The Buddhists gave new blankets to every patient, several bars of soap, boxes of matches, and a cash gift. It is not surprising that Christianity makes such slow progress in Thailand. One thing that has helped me forget my shame and bitterness over these poor gifts has been the abundance of love, gratitude, and gifts that I have received from the patients. These poor folks have so little for themselves and yet many have scrimped and saved out of their meager savings to buy me a present. Nine of the carvers together made me an elephant pushing a log. Another carver gave me a standing elephant. The leprosy church gave me a tray. Surin, Twee, and Mungkorn gave me a diary and some cloth. Boonlurt gave me a lacquer water bowl and the Bukers gave me a brass temple gong. I do not know what to do with these gifts. They are so superior to those that the Christian groups have given to the leprosy patients that it seems wrong for me to accept them. And yet if I do not accept them I shall only hurt the people who have sacrificed so much to give them to me.

February 15, 1953

Today there was an urgent request sent down from one of the nearby leprosy villages, thirty miles away, asking us to come and get a very sick old man. I took two of my friends in the "powerful" utilivan and we jolted along at about twenty-five miles an hour. Though driving the little English Ford is almost torture, I enjoyed being out in the country again.

The poor old fellow has been a leper for many years and was so weak now that he was unable to walk. He climbed onto one of the villagers' back and was carried to the car. I was reminded of one of the pathetic scenes in the leprosy movie made in the colony years ago. It is always a little touching to me to see how unemotional and outwardly callous lepers appear and yet how tenderly and kindly they help one another when in need. By the time we arrived back at the colony the old fellow appeared badly shaken up. In time, however, and with treatment he improved.

A funny little episode happened in town a week ago. One of the mission families was visited by a burglar while their watchman was, as usual, asleep. The neighbors' watchman heard the prowler and gave the alarm, whereupon the sleeping watchman got up and in his drowsy, bewildered state graciously opened the gate of the compound so that the burglar could leave. He figured that it was his job to keep the compound free of prowlers and therefore the only thing to do was to let the prowler out. The fact that the prowler carried an armful of loot with him was, apparently, beside the point.

March 15, 1953

Last week I rode with some friends to Chiengrai and spent four days there. The first ninety miles north to Fang was the same beautiful road that I have traveled before. Just south of Fang, however, we turned off to the east and did not see another village for almost seventy-five miles. Several years ago a bulldozer plowed through the jungle and over the mountains to make a road. And that is what the road is today, an unimproved bulldozer trail. All day long we puffed up mountains and then dashed down the other side and splashed through small streams and then back up another mountain and down the other side. There is supposed to be a maintenance crew at work clearing out landslides and trimming off fallen trees but no one seemed to be in any particular hurry to do this work. The scenery was superb. Sometimes we would look off from a ridge over miles and miles of jungle, and then at other times the vegetation was so thick that it looked as if walls of green had been built along the side of the road. This area is inhabited by tigers, leopards, wild elephants, and the usual variety of small game. They were scared away because my friend was so worried about meeting another car around the hairpin bends that he blew his horn almost continuously. While I was in Chiengrai I went to see a Karen village. The Karens are the largest tribal group in Southeast Asia. In order to reach the village dry, we removed our trousers and waded waist deep across a wide river. I also visited the Overbrook Presbyterian Mission hospital and the Experimental Farm a few miles out of town. And then went back

56

into the jungle and watched the elephants work one morning. I am really a glutton for elephants: I can watch them all day.

I returned to Chiengmai, just in time to welcome a movie crew that had come to make a color film about leprosy work in Thailand. There were two cameramen and the director—Alan Shilen, who owned the film company. He had been commissioned by the American Leprosy Mission.

I remember that I was really excited about the filming of the work in Chiengmai, not only because it seemed an excellent opportunity for showing people at home what a terrible disease leprosy is, but also because I got to observe the techniques of movie-making.

The most surprising thing for me, was that the director worked out in advance every shot he intended to take. I had imagined that when shooting a documentary film of this kind one wandered about with a camera and photographed things spontaneously. I soon realized how impractical such a method would be. The waste of film would be fantastic.

Shilen's technique was to walk around the colony with a note-book taking in the atmosphere of the place and noting down the essential "shots." Then he visualized the film in his imagination and planned it shot by shot—a close-up of this, a long shot of that, and so on. When he had planned the whole thing the cameramen shot according to his instructions and all the snippets of film— usually not filmed in any kind of sequence—were later edited into a continuous narrative and dialogue was added. It was a most instructive few days for me, and the crew was very good about answering my questions and explaining techniques.

Dr. Buker was more interested in the content of the film than in its technique and I remember his saying, "I am sure you are making a technically good film, Alan, but it won't say anything. I have watched you at work and you haven't photographed one single bad case of leprosy. When people at home see your film they still won't know what leprosy can do to a person. If you want to film the truth, film the toeless feet, the clawed hands, the sunken noses, the ulcers, and the sores. Film the misery of many of the patients. Try to show their bitterness and despair."

But Alan explained that the American Leprosy Mission had insisted that the film should be "horror-free." He had been instructed to make a happy film about happy lepers in a happy leprosy colony. Apparently the American Leprosy Mission felt that it would be easier to raise money with a happy film than a tragic one.

Dr. Buker did persuade Alan to film some of the badly disfigured patients, but I noticed when I saw the film in America a few months later that all the "horror shots" had been edited out. The highlight of the film was a sequence about a woman who had been a dancer in her youth and had performed before the Chiengmai royalty. This sequence provided plenty of local color and was shot in the grounds of the U.S. Consulate, which at one time had been the Royal Palace. The story told how the girl had contracted leprosy, gone to the McKean Colony, and been cured. It showed her as an old woman, happy and well in the security of the colony. But it omitted showing her terrible disfigurement and pointing out that someone had been partially destroyed in the prime of her womanhood and had been forced to spend four decades in a leper colony, cut off from all normal contact with the outside world. It glossed over the misery and pain, the despair and isolation. The film told only half the story—the happier half.

I cannot agree with the American Leprosy Mission that as far as leprosy is concerned all is now well in the world. In my opinion their attempts to make leprosy appear as innocuous as tuberculosis —a disease that can be cured and leave the patient a normal person—are doing irreparable harm to leprosy work. All is far from being well. Leprosy is one of the most terrible diseases to afflict human beings, and the seriousness of the problem is staggering considered in terms of statistics alone. Between ¼ per cent to 1 per cent of the Afro-Asian population is suffering from leprosy, and there does not seem to be any noticeable decrease in this percentage. In fact at an American Leprosy Mission conference conducted in the U.S. Public Health leprosy hospital in Carville, Louisiana, in March 1961, I heard the director of the hospital, Dr. Johnstone, say that leprosy is one of the fastest-increasing diseases in the world today. This may be explained by the advance made in the treatment of malaria and yaws and other diseases. People who escape these diseases live longer and are thus given time to show the symptoms of leprosy.

On page 3 of the January 10, 1966, issue of *The American Medical Association News* the following statement appeared: "Leprosy is twice as prevalent in the world today as it was ten years ago, reported Paul W. Brand, MD, British surgeon who has worked with leprosy victims in India. Dr. Brand, writing in *Rehabilitation Record*, said that the disease 'is not being controlled,' and that about three fourths of the fifteen million people in the world who have leprosy are not being treated for it."

Happy, sentimental films may make members of church groups and charitable organizations feel good themselves, but they do little to alleviate the suffering of most of the world's lepers. I believe that the world must be shocked into a realization that leprosy is a terrible problem, and the techniques used to solicit help should show it as it really is.

So far in this story I have stressed my own experiences—my daily life. This has been deliberate because I enjoyed my travels and my work at the McKean Colony and I have tried to show that working among lepers can be a happy and interesting life so that anyone reading my story who has the time and a little money may feel that he or she, too, would find the work worthwhile. But it must never be forgotten that bad cases of leprosy, and there are hundreds of thousands of them, look and feel wretched and ugly.

The fear of leprosy is so great in most communities that often people who contract it either are forced out of their villages and left to fend for themselves or, if they are deeply loved by their families, are simply locked away—the skeleton in the family closet.

A year later I was to see examples of this fear in Angsela, a coastal village south of Chonburi.

The village is built over the sea on stilts. In many ways it is a tropical paradise—palm trees, a silvery moon, and the soft shushing of the waves. But there is a great deal of leprosy in the village, most of it carefully hidden away. As I walked along the planks connecting the houses Surin said, "People say there is a sick man hidden in that end house. No one has seen him for many years and no one can remember him dying. He will be a leper."

"How do you know?"

"I just know. We will try and visit him." We called at the wooden house and Surin explained that he had heard that there was a sick man living there. He did not mention the leprosy. We had some medicines, he explained, and would like to visit the man.

At first the old woman who came to the door denied that anyone lived in the house except her sons, their wives and children, all of whom were well. But Surin persisted, and I suspect that he told the woman I was a foreign doctor who would go away the same day and never return and betray her secret. After a long conversation she let us into the wooden shack and pointed toward a small door at the far end. We opened it and entered a dark hut no bigger than a broom cupboard. When our eyes became accustomed to the dim light filtering in through cracks in the wall, we could see a man huddled in front of us. Surin spoke to him and bent down. The man was an advanced case of leprosy. He had been alone for so long that he could hardly speak and he was more dead than alive. He breathed and, presumably, he ate from plates of food pushed into the room. He was also fairly clean, and we gathered that the old woman or her family helped him occasionally to wash himself. His lavatory was a hole in the floor opening into the sea below. He did not know how long he had been in the room, but Surin guessed that he had had leprosy for at least twenty years and had been confined from the time the first signs of the disease appeared.

There was little we could do for him. Even if we left him DDS medicine, there was no guarantee that he would take the correct dosage and he was really too far advanced for any effective treatment. And so we left him where he was, knowing that nothing could be done. Had he been taken to a doctor years before he would have been spared a lifetime of solitary confinement and his disease might have been arrested. Surin told me that there are hundreds of these hidden cases throughout Thailand. Their families are afraid to admit leprosy because the stigma can prevent the children from marrying and can even prevent the whole family from having normal social relations with the community. As they dare not admit leprosy and the signs are obvious, the only thing they can do is to lock the patient away at the first sign and hope that evasive replies to questions will satisfy neighborhood curiosity. Sometimes this fear is so great that the patient is told to leave the house and disappear. As we left the wooden shack the old woman said to Surin, "There is a girl. Under the pier. Out there." And she pointed to where a pier stretched out from the huts farther along the village. We walked toward it and climbed down from the wooden catwalk onto the sand below. A few yards ahead of us at the tide mark we could see a girl between fifteen and twenty-five—it was difficult to guess her age—sitting among the refuse and detritus left by the retreating sea.

The girl was a leper. The crippling and disfigurement had not yet ravaged her completely but the depredations of the disease showed on her face and feet. The muscles in her hands were beginning to tighten and the clawlike appearance was just becoming noticeable. She muttered to Surin that she had been forced to leave her village several years before when she was thirteen and that she had wandered for some time until she had found this shelter beneath the wooden pier in Angsela. The people of the village, she said, threw her scraps of food and rice wrapped in banana leaves but she dared not venture into the village for fear they would chase her out and she would have nowhere to go. More than this, Surin could not find out, for she spoke in a lifeless disinterested tone. She had lost all hope and no longer thought about herself as a person at all. She accepted that she was a thing that needed to eat and sleep, no more. Whatever regrets and despair she had known at first were now apparently forgotten. She was no longer a human being with desires and hopes, thoughts of love, family, or friends. She had become less responsive than a stray mangy cat.

Meeting these two people, the hidden man and the outcast girl, convinced me that it is not enough to treat the physical effects of leprosy. The patients' minds must be given equal if not more attention. They must be helped back to normality, made to understand that they are ordinary people with a handicap that can be overcome in the same way that a blind or lame person can overcome his disability.

Leprosy is not just a medical problem, it is a social problem as well. It is begging the whole question to say that with DDS, the wonder drug, the leprosy problem is all but solved and that the only need is to pay for the free distribution of the drug.

Modern drugs cannot make a disfigured leper whole again: they can do nothing to return him to normal society. Only the education of society itself will enable the arrested and disfigured leper to return and be accepted in the way that a cured TB patient is. And the eradication of fear in simple village societies cannot be achieved overnight. It will take many years before the arrested lepers are welcomed back to their villages. In the meantime some way must be found to enable them to lead a normal life. Something must be done to prevent them from becoming living dead, institutionalized in hospitals for life, hidden in back rooms of houses, or hobbling about the countryside begging for enough food to stay alive. Something must be done to help them feel that they are real people capable of experiencing all the joys of being alive.

Chapter 4

It was now April 1953. I had been away from home for a year and I realized that happy though I was at McKean I could not stay on indefinitely. I had no official position in the organization and not being a doctor or a missionary I wasn't likely to get one. I was no more than the man who came to dinner and stayed for a year.

Dr. and Mrs. Buker continued to make me welcome and I felt like an adopted son, but it was obvious to us all that the time had come for me to think of my own future. If I intended to spend my life working with leprosy patients I had to join an organization or start a project somewhere on my own. I decided to return home, make a little money from my movie business for a few months, and see what developed.

On the day I left the colony, April 12, between four and five hundred patients lined the road to the gate to say good-by. I was moved more than I can bear to recall. It was as if I had actually done something to help them, instead of having merely lived in the place and done odd jobs for Dr. Buker. Thinking back on it now, I suspect that their appreciation was not for any tangible good that I had done them—for I had done nothing—but for my having lived among them. I realize now that one of the most important factors in the rehabilitation of leprosy patients is friendly, normal contact with unafflicted people. When he is not rejected the leper can better adjust to his unfortunate condition.

I returned home by sea via Japan and Vancouver. My parents were in Minneapolis to meet me and we drove back to Albert Lea. For the first few weeks I did nothing but visit family and friends and talk about my experiences. I think only my parents believed most of the things I said. Travelers' tales are always fairly tall and no doubt mine seemed taller than most. A year's stay in a leper colony was not the usual idea of an Oriental tour.

Soon I started up the movie business again and the state of my bank account gradually improved. At this time, too, I was in local demand as a speaker. Albert Lea is full of church groups of one denomination or another, and they are always on the lookout for a speaker. My experiences were out of the ordinary and I was happy to talk about them. It seemed to me that if more people knew about leprosy more would be done to help the patients.

From the small church groups I graduated to such larger groups as Rotarians and Lions Clubs. From these groups I sometimes received a little money to send back to Dr. Buker. I also imported from McKean some teak carvings which I sold to raise money for Dr. Buker's work. One evening my father said to me, "You cannot spend the rest of your life talking to church groups and showing movies during the summer, Bob. Hadn't you better think about your future?" My father was right, of course, but I could not make a decision to start a real career. At the back of my mind there was the idea that I ought to return to Thailand. At the same time I knew I could not return to live under the old arrangement. If I did return I had to have some backing and a purpose. I could not spend my life drifting about the McKean Colony.

Then, just as I was coming to a decision to forget the lepers and to take a job teaching school, I got a letter from the American Leprosy Mission. They were having their booth in the annual National Sunday School Convention in Minneapolis and wrote to ask if I would care to help and display the carvings made by the McKean lepers. If I cared to talk about my experiences to the groups of visiting Sunday-school teachers, this would also be very useful, they said. I accepted the invitation and for about a week I stood at the booth talking and handing out American Leprosy Mission literature. At the end of the convention, Miss Lulu Ervin, the head of the American Leprosy Mission Chicago office, asked if I would like to work for the Mission as a kind of field representative in the Midwest. Although this was a far cry from working with lepers, it seemed a worthwhile thing to do, and so I agreed and moved into a cheap hotel in Chicago between the night-club area and the slums. Using the hotel as a base I traveled through Kentucky, Indiana, Wisconsin, Minnesota, and Iowa, talking to groups and handing out literature.

The only thing that worried me was the American Leprosy Mission literature: it was all so nice—so cheerful and optimistic. Just give your dollar or your dime, it seemed to say, and this rather nasty but not really terrible disease will be completely cured and removed from the face of the earth. And the tragic thing was, it seemed to me, that the American Leprosy Mission workers were the dupes of their own literature. They really believed that leprosy was not really all that bad. Most of them had never seen a leprosy patient, and although they meant well they had no real conception of the disease. The policy behind the fund-raising activities seemed to be to avoid shocking anyone. They did not even call leprosy by its name but referred to it instead as Hansen's disease.

I could not go along with this policy. And when I came across articles in *The Star*, the newspaper of the American leprosy colony at Carville, Louisiana, saying that leprosy does not really disfigure and that it is not such a terrible disease as some people try to make out, I became really worried. Although I understood that the idea of the American Leprosy Mission was to try to avoid the stigma attached to leprosy, I could not agree that the problem would be solved by turning away from the facts. Gradually I introduced into my talks my own experiences with leprosy and said exactly how I felt about it. I showed an 8-millimeter film which I had taken of some of the McKean patients. I talked about the fear

65

of leprosy—the outcasts and the patients locked in back rooms. I explained in detail what the disease could do to a man or a woman. And I believe I was right to do this. My audience seemed to appreciate the truth, for again and again people came up to me and said, "We have heard speakers before but this is the first time we have ever heard exactly what leprosy is."

The months passed and I became increasingly dissatisfied with the way my life was going. I was doing nothing to help the leprosy patients, and I could not get back to them through the American Leprosy Mission because it has no workers in the field. Gradually I developed the idea of returning to Thailand to make an honest documentary film in color about the disease. Such a film, I thought, might shock people into a true realization of what leprosy is.

My movie business was still bringing in money and I was able to buy the additional equipment and film. I thought I already had enough experience and knowledge—thanks to the patience of the film unit at McKean—to make a technically acceptable film. I wrote to Dr. Buker and asked him what he thought about this idea. He was, as usual, full of encouragement and I could think of no good reason for not going ahead with the project.

Then a few days before I was due to leave I was asked to give a talk at the Trinity Lutheran Church in Albert Lea. Their speaker had canceled at the last moment and they wanted me as a fill-in.

During my talk I mentioned for the first time the possibilities of starting leprosy rehabilitation villages. In my naïve and inexperienced way I said that it ought to be possible to start such a village with as little as $500 to $1000. One of the audience, a fairly senior member of the church, stood up and said that if I would start a village he was sure the church group could raise enough money to support me in the work. No actual sum of money was mentioned but I had the impression that they would somehow find enough to found the village and add a few dollars for me to live on.

I had never felt so encouraged. I had saved up a few thousand dollars of my own during the year, enough to get me back to Thailand, make my film, and then continue with a project on my own with the support from the church. At that time I could ask for nothing more, and I left for Thailand in high spirits.

When I got back to Chiengmai I had a fine reunion with Dr. and Mrs. Buker and my other friends at the colony, particularly Surin and Twee. I arrived in February just a month before the Bukers were due to go on a year's leave. The first job, therefore, was to make as much of the film as possible while Dr. Buker was available to give advice and set up a few operations for me to film.

Dr. Buker said that I could not have arrived at a better time. While he was on leave the colony would not have an administrator until Rob Marvin, another Presbyterian missionary, arrived in September. The medical work would be looked after by Dr. Ed McDaniels of the McCormick Hospital in Chiengmai, but there would be no one to keep an eye on the administration of the colony. Dr. Buker asked me if I would stay on as a kind of unofficial supervisor. I agreed, of course, although I felt even then that my unofficial status would probably cause problems.

There was no point in bringing up problems before they occurred and so we agreed that I would stay on, finish my film, act as a supervisor until Rob Marvin arrived, and then go out and start a village with the support of the McKean Colony and the Trinity Church in Albert Lea. Everything seemed to be working out well.

As things turned out, the time at the colony after Dr. Buker left was a miserable period. I had good friends in Surin and Twee but I did not get on real well with some of the other missionaries. The details of this time are no longer important but the mission groups concerned with the McKean Leprosarium seemed to divide into two camps, one of which objected to Dr. Buker's policy and

67

everything he had done. After months of arguments and recriminations it was decided that Dr. Buker would not return to Thailand and that the colony would be run by Dr. Chinda Singhanet a Thai doctor of considerable influence and position not only in Chiengmai but in the Thailand Presbyterian movement. As a protégé and supporter of Dr. Buker, I found myself *persona non grata* at the McKean Colony and was eventually asked, in no uncertain terms, to leave.

When I left I took with me, to a piece of land north of the city, twelve of the McKean patients including Surin and Twee. It was unfortunate that we had to start our village in this way without the help and good will of the Leprosy Mission, but when I think back on it, perhaps it was all to the good. I was so infuriated by the attitude of the new administration that I was more than ever determined to make the village a success. It is likely that my driving force in the founding of Trinity Village was a particularly unholy kind of pride. Dr. Buker had believed in me and said that what I wanted to do was not only possible but sensible. I had to succeed if I was not to let him down.

I had, of course, realized that a break with McKean was coming, and several weeks before I finally was asked to leave, Surin and I had concluded negotiations for a piece of land seventy-eight kilometers to the north.

We had found this land on June 9, 1955. We had spent a day walking through the jungle in the Chiengdao area. Our routine was to go down a logging trail to the river and then walk. The jungle was hot, humid, and steamy. From time to time we got lost and had to retrace our steps to the river and start out again. At first we found nothing that was worth settling a village on. Then later in the afternoon we stumbled on a track that continued through a maze of vines and brought us out to a partly cleared valley within a stone's throw from a bend in the river. A small part of the area was already under cultivation and we found out that a couple of families from a distant village had been trying to raise rice on it. We went to visit these families, since they held no more than squatters' rights to the land and had put little work into it. They were pleased to collect money for it. Their village headman was agreeable to the sale and the local provincial officer had no objections either. Thus for $325 we acquired title to a well-situated piece of land with nearby water supply. A month later the deeds were finally approved, and on August 9 we left the McKean Colony to start a new life together at Trinity Village, Chiengdao.

August 9, 1955

Today I am as stiff and sore as if I had just finished the first football practice of the season. What ought to have been a routine day of hauling up personal belongings and equipment to the site of Trinity Village turned out to be twelve hours of chaos. The bus arrived at McKean Colony on time and we loaded everything: bedrolls, pots and pans, tools, forty turkeys, twenty-five ducks, two hundred chickens, several geese, and, strapped to the top, three pigs in bamboo cases. According to good Thai custom, about fifteen extra people also climbed aboard the bus. They had asked permission from nobody but simply figured that if a bus was paid for they might as well go along for the ride.

On our way through town we picked up a couple of sacks of rice and some meat and vegetables. On the long drive to Chiengdao the bus overheated and the water boiled away frequently. About every ten miles we had to stop to refill the radiator. Fortunately it is the rainy season and nearly everywhere people are flooding their paddy land, and so it was not difficult for us to find water. The driver was intensely worried about the mountains and averaged only about ten miles an hour for the last twenty miles.

Eventually we reached Chiengdao village and all thirty of us had dinner in various little restaurants in the market. Then we continued another ten miles or so to our land. Here our troubles really began. Twee had brought a group up a few days ahead of us to work on the bridges, but because of the abundant rainfall the grass had grown terrifically and had blotted out the track in places. The grass was three or four feet high and the leaves and branches of trees hung so low with the weight of raindrops that the road looked as if it had never been used. At first the driver refused to leave the main road. Eventually we persuaded him and he started down the trail only to stop completely when he came to the first bridge. Twee had cut new trees and fixed it quite adequately, but the bus crew refused to cross and we had to unload everything right there in the middle of the jungle at least a mile from the site of our village. We carried everything on foot the rest of the way. Although the ground was reasonably firm the surface soon became slippery from our scuffling. As I slogged along the wet, humid trail with a box on my shoulder and trying to dodge the slim branches that slashed at my face and body, I kept thinking of the Tarzan movies and how thrilling it had looked to see a heavily laden caravan snake through the jungle. How different reality. This was hot, hard, unglamorous work.

Second only to Surin is Twee. His inborn talents for leadership are not at all diminished by his severe disfigurement. Twee contracted leprosy when he was a boy of twelve and shortly thereafter both of his parents died. He spent a brief time with relatives, but as his disease progressed they grew increasingly afraid of him and sent him to the government colony in Phra Pa Daeng. After a few years of assisting in the kitchens there and of watching his face and hands slowly deteriorate, he decided to try McKean Colony in the north. He escaped under the fence and found his way to the railroad yards where he climbed into a northbound freight train.

For three weeks he edged his way north on freight trains. He ate what scraps he could beg or find and he slept under any available shelter. The police would chase Twee off the train whenever they discovered him and he occasionally had stones thrown at him but he kept sneaking into other trains and kept persistently on his way to Chiengmai.

The night he arrived in Chiengmai he curled up in a dark alley to sleep, only to be awakened and robbed of what few belongings he had by a couple of other beggars. The next day he arrived at McKean Colony with barely the shirt on his back.

Twee was always fascinated by books and read whatever he could get his hands on. By the time I met him he had already managed to pick up enough English so that he was able to read books in English and was greatly widening his knowledge of the world. He developed into one of the better teachers at McKean for the school maintained for leprosy children. Later Twee attended the Christian Missionary Alliance Bible School for leprosy patients in Khonkaen and he returned to become one of the most active Christian teachers in our village.

August 21, 1955

I have been too busy to write anything for the last few weeks but now things are getting a little easier. The fellows have cleared a fairly large area already and built a bamboo hut with a leaf roof for me. I am finding the work very hard, I am afraid. The site of our village is covered with small trees and shrubs laced together with vines. In no time at all I have got blisters and calluses on my hands and my back aches and I am usually wet, hot, tired, and discouraged. The puny little guys with the leprosy hands and feet do not seem to notice the hardship. They keep on singing and working as if there were nothing to it. They hack down the trees and then grub out the roots and burn them. Their feet are wet all the time and their clothing rarely dries out. They slip and fall in the mud and bruise themselves, and their stiff leprous fingers crack and bleed. But their spirit is marvelous and they keep right on working without any urging. At night I sleep on a bamboo mat in good jungle style. I drop off to sleep fairly quickly, but it is not long before the hardness of the mat bruises me into wakefulness. Painfully I roll over onto my other side or onto my back or stomach in an attempt to ease a screaming muscle. When I wake up I hear lizards race by hunting for bugs and mosquitoes to eat. These lizards are harmless to men but look horrible and detract considerably from the comfort of my bedroom. My house is, of course, only a bamboo floor suspended about four feet off the ground on poles, with a few woven bamboo mats for walls, and a roof made of leaves tied together in rows to make shingles. When I take a bath I go to the river, and when I go to the bathroom I use the jungle. Drinking water is boiled river water which is both dirty-looking and lukewarm. I have never seen anyone in the worst of slums live in a poorer house than mine, and yet I am surprised how comfortable and contented I am here.

Surin's wife, Lai, moved up here on Friday and brought the gibbon with her. [The gibbon, a pet of Dr. and Mrs. Buker's, had been given to me when they left for America.] On the bus from the colony he vomited continuously. He is such a spindly little fellow that she was amazed to see how much he had inside him. As soon as he set foot to the ground he was well and happy again.

When we were unpacking some things we found a scorpion and a centipede inside. Though their stings will not kill an average adult, they are extremely painful. We killed both creatures easily, and they did not seem to disturb anyone except me. It never ceases to amaze me how much less dangerous and thrilling things are in real life than in stories. For example, this morning while one of the fellows was visiting me he noticed a snake curled up asleep in one of the little food baskets hanging from the lower end of my roof, just a couple of feet from where I eat my breakfast. The snake would not leave the basket and kept poking his head over the side. The fellows finally got a cover onto the basket and took it outside where they dumped the snake and killed it.

The basket held only about two quarts but the snake measured nearly five feet when we stretched it out. The men told me that it was deadly poisonous but no one knew the English name for it.

I should complete an outdoor toilet tomorrow, a needless luxury and a horrible waste of time in the opinion of my Thai friends. A dormitory-style house for the fellows should be finished in a week or so, after which we plan to dig a well. Most of my time for the next few weeks will probably be spent in cutting and clearing underbrush. Although this is a hard life it is a healthy one and I feel extremely well.

September 5, 1955

It is peaceful and restful here. The scenery is truly beautiful. From my house I look out across the cleared area and rice paddies toward the dense jungle on the mountain side about a quarter of a mile distant. The river is about a hundred yards east of my cabin but because of the still uncut underbrush I cannot see it from where I sit. During the last few days I have done very little work myself. In clearing off a couple of hundred feet of jungle I developed a few new blisters which I am now waiting to clear up. (Broken blisters become infected quickly in this climate.) The last few days I have spent most of my time just sitting back enjoying the whole atmosphere of the village. During the day we can hear and sometimes see gibbons frolicking in the nearby trees. During the night we hear all sorts of bird and animal life, but I am not jungle-bred enough to know which sounds belong to which creatures.

By the flickering light of the fire or kerosene lantern I play a little game. The leaves in my roof will crackle and whisper when something moves through them and I speculate as to what will eventually stick its head out and where. There are all sorts of lizards and snakes to surprise me. When the head does poke through, I then speculate as to the type and length of body attached behind. Since I don't want to ruin my leaf shingles with unnecessary probing either I can wait for the creature to expose itself completely or I can drop off to sleep and dream up my own ending.

This is not quite the jungle life you see in movies. I had previously imagined living in a hut nestling under towering trees and overgrown with vines. I imagined monkeys and other wild animals coming to my doorstep, and believed that every time I left my house I would have to hack out a narrow trail. The fact is that no such a place exists in this area. The first thing that anyone does when he builds a house in the jungle is to cut back all the undergrowth as far as possible to ensure safety from snakes and other creatures. Insects and scorpions and centipedes would overrun a place if the brush wasn't cleared. At the closest point to my house the jungle is about twenty yards away and I know that to increase my security I must cut it back at least another twenty yards all around.

We now have twenty-one people in our village and expect four or five more to arrive today, if advance reports are true. Every day or so another patient straggles in from the McKean Leprosarium. Most of the fellows living here now have been classified as troublemakers and thieves by the administrators at McKean. But I am really proud and pleased with them. Troublemakers they may be but they are men with spirit and initiative who are not afraid to soil their hands working in the jungle.

September 14, 1955

Time goes by very quickly. It has been six weeks since the first fellows moved onto the land. This week we have finished their large dormitory-style bamboo-and-leaf building which should adequately shelter thirty-five people. We cleared a place halfway up

74

the mountain side and put the building there in the shadows of towering teak trees. It has a long roof that slants almost to the ground on each side. It has no walls. The center aisle, which is about ten feet wide, is merely a dirt floor and provides the sleeping area. It is not elaborate but everybody is very pleased with it.

Two hundred more pineapple plants were bought today bringing our total to four hundred. Garden space is being cleared for vegetables and the rice planted by the squatters will be harvested in a few days. The empty paddy field will provide more space for gardens.

Some of the fellows are cutting and dragging more bamboo out of the jungle and using it to construct fences for our chickens, ducks, geese, and turkeys. This is no easy task. The heavy rains have made all the jungle trails very slippery. To get the bamboo, the fellows have to go a long distance up and down and around the mountain terrain. They cut poles about thirty feet long and drag them out four at a time, one end on their shoulders and the other end dragging. The men frequently slip and fall and the weight of the bamboo pushes them along through the mud and slime. They laugh at one another and as soon as possible struggle back up on their crippled feet, readjust their loads with those stiff hands, and continue on their way. I continue to be amazed at their spirit.

September 19, 1955

Trinity Village is gradually beginning to look more like a village than a small cleared hole in the jungle. Now that the large dormitory is finished and all the pigs and poultry have been moved into permanent bamboo pens, the men are spending most of their time clearing away more jungle for gardens and selecting sites for their own personal cabins. Every day therefore now brings about a noticeable change in the appearance of the village.

We cannot buy vegetables of any kind in the Chiengdao village market so until our own gardens begin to produce we have to go to Chiengmai by bus nearly every week to get supplies. The last time I was there I thought about what a wonderful experience I am having and how my attitudes have changed. Using Oriental toilet facilities now seems to be quite natural to me. Waiting hours for a bus also seems quite normal to me now, and I can wait as patiently as the rest of the local people. And eating only rice, curry, and noodles also seems to be part of my life. Even trying to evade the mud churned up by water buffaloes while I am taking a bath in the river and living under a leaf roof in a house with no furniture seem natural enough. I had experienced many inconveniences before and endured them for a few days at a time, but I always had a haven of American culture to flee to when things got too bad. Sometimes, in China, it was the Army-requisitioned resort hotels or barracks. Later on, at the McKean Leprosarium, it was Dr. Buker's home or Western-style hotels. There was always someplace with an American atmosphere when I wanted it. But now I have nowhere to go and I find that I am eating, sleeping, traveling, and working in local fashion in company with the local people all the time and that I am really learning a very great deal. With no escape I have been forced to accept many things. And the strangest part of it all is how comfortable and adequate an existence it is. At the same time I think there is a kind of monotony beginning to settle over our village. I suppose it is only natural that the fine edge should wear off after weeks of hard work. A number of the men are bringing their wives and children to live here now and this should help to liven the place up a little. Everybody still works well, and yet I think there is a spark missing somewhere. Perhaps it's in me. Things that stimulated and interested me a while back are now not of very great interest. Perhaps I am becoming a victim of loneliness. I see all sorts of things going on and many people busily engaged in the everyday tasks of living, and yet I am really not a part of it. I wish there were some way in which I could identify myself with these people, some way in which I could make myself feel that Trinity Village was as much my home as theirs. I think part of my feeling of being outside everything is caused by the language barrier. At the McKean Leprosarium I was just getting used to holding simple conversations in Thai. But here all the people speak Lao, which is a northern dialect of Thai and very different. Outside of the villages, the Chinese merchants and restaurant keepers all speak their own dialects of Chinese, none of which I can understand.

However, nature is always a consolation, and one of the nicest things here in Trinity is the privilege of watching the sunsets. Usually, deep in the jungle, you cannot see the sunset at all. With my house on a hill I have a splendid view. The colors of the sky are indeed beautiful, but it is the way the jungle becomes dark and dim while the sky continues to retain a light glow that I find so enthralling. During the day I am not too conscious of the outline of the mountain and the jungle. But at sunset giant treetops stand out against the sky next to blunt mountain ridges and sharp peaks. Slight valleys or clefts in the mountains become very noticeable. The sky appears even brighter as thousands of stars come out and begin to twinkle softly. The jungle gets darker and darker and suddenly the symphony of small jungle noises rises to a crescendo. In some ways the jungle is peaceful after dark, in others terribly frightening.

October 12, 1955

Last night we had trouble from the jungle. For some time I have been hearing tales of wild animals and what might happen if they came to the village. A hunter from a neighboring village shot a wild pig a week or so ago and killed a deer. I imagined that his activity and the noise from our growing community would

77

frighten any wild animals away from our village, but last night, just after midnight, something jumped into our poultry pen and killed one of the large geese. When the other birds began screeching Twee went out to see what the trouble was. The only thing he could find was the half-eaten remains of a goose and a lot of worried fowls crowded into one side of the pen. From the marks on the goose and on the ground the fellows suggested it must have been a leopard. I am afraid he will return for another easy meal since he had such good luck this time. We have no gun of any kind, but some of the fellows are making crossbows which they think will be sufficient. Personally, I am not so sure. The wife of one of the men is a Mao tribe girl and she says she can make a trap to catch it. But I do not think anybody wants her to make this trap because we are all frightened that if we do catch it we won't know how to hold it or kill it.

The last time the fellows were in the jungle they saw a large black- and orange-banded krait, but they did not care to try and kill it. A krait is a powerful snake and deadly poisonous. Fortunately it is not too aggressive. The one they saw was, they tell me, at least eight feet long. I had been in the jungle with them that day but had come home before they met the snake.

Some of these jungle trails are strenuous to walk along. They twist and turn over and around outcroppings of rock and fallen logs. Long sections are often so overgrown with vines and brush that the trail becomes a tunnel. I cannot say I enjoy crawling along these tunnels, humped over and scraping my back on gnarled vines. All the air is cut off, and the sweat runs down into my eyes, and when I look up to see a little bit of sky and see nothing but a twisted mat of vines, I wonder where I would go or what I would do if I met a wild pig or a tiger head-on in one of these tunnels. Whenever possible I return from my trips into the jungle by way of the river. Surin and I walk down the center of the river stripped of our clothing and holding it over our heads to keep it dry. The river has a very fast current which really pushes one along. Sometimes I bang my knees on a rock or sand bar or become tangled on a submerged fallen tree. Nevertheless I prefer this way of traveling to the jungle tunnels.

Another thing about the jungle is that you can hear rain coming a mile away. This roar of the water on the leaves gives you five minutes or more to get under shelter. Sometimes you can hear the shower change direction, and sometimes you hear it passing you by on one side or the other. When you first hear this distant roar coming closer and closer it is rather frightening because it exaggerates the degree of the storm.

One of the hunters from a nearby village uses an old flintlock musket which looks as if it's at least two hundred years old. It is almost laughable to see him carrying it out hunting. But he still brings back game.

October 29, 1955

Our leopard has not returned so maybe our goose gave him indigestion. But the fellows have made the acquaintance of a couple of other rather unwelcome creatures. They met a huge king cobra in the nearby jungle the other day but hurried by without fraternizing.

About a week ago while Dao, the Thai man married to a Mao girl, was working in the garden near the river he came face to face with another cobra. The cobra hooded and backed up in fright and Dao dropped his knife and retreated also. Then both became brave and charged. With the help of a bamboo pole Dao laid the cobra out dead. It was about five feet long. The people in this area believe that if you beat a snake but do not completely kill it, it will eventually find you and kill you. To make sure this cobra was really dead, they drove a stake through its head and pinned it to the ground.

The other day while I was walking to our village from the highway I came upon a group of monkeys playing in the trees along the road. The monkeys in this area are gun-shy from being shot at, and they do not usually allow anyone to get very close to them. [Monkeys are killed for food. It was quite an experience for me the first time I saw one of the patients dip down into a steaming pot of stewlike curry and calmly begin chewing on a disturbingly human-looking hand and forearm. He described the monkey meat as delicious but a bit tough.] You can often see monkeys in distant trees safely out of rifle range, but you rarely see them so close. These had not heard me as I was alone. We stared at each other for a few minutes, all afraid to make the first move. Then soundlessly they slipped down the tall trees and disappeared like magic into the brush. If they had fled by way of the treetops I could have watched their route for quite a distance.

Occasionally a gibbon or two will come to the edge of the jungle and call to my little gibbon. However, the gibbon I have has been a pet for so long that he does not even recognize these visitors as relations of his. He has got loose from his chain a couple of times but never tried to go into the jungle. He much prefers to come into the house and snoop for food and generally tear things up. Every morning he wakes me by reaching his arm through the bamboo wall mat and shaking my mosquito net. He keeps at it until he feels confident I won't slip back into sleep again. My gibbon is also pretty good about giving the alarm if any snakes come close to the house. His whoops are penetrating and unmistakable.

Last week we bought two oxen and an oxcart. The oxen seem to be strong and the cart sturdy enough. We have used it to haul a few things so far, but mostly we use the oxen to keep down the grass along the paths.

At present the fellows are digging a well, I guess I should say they are digging a hole which we hope will become a well. If we find a good well we plan to build a storage tank and install a pump and water system for irrigating our fields. If we can raise crops during the dry season I am certain we can make some money.

November 22, 1955

I thought I was going to freeze to death this morning. The winter season has now come and the temperatures have dropped to about fifty degrees. It is amazing how cold fifty degrees seems here. During the night as the air cools off a heavy fog forms so that in the morning it is impossible to see as far as twenty feet. Getting out of bed, dressing, and eating breakfast in this cloud feels like living in the Arctic. By about eight-thirty the sun has dried up the fog and everything is back to tropical temperatures again.

It is nearly a month since I last wrote in this book and things in Trinity Village do not look too different. The only noticeable difference is in the size and neatness of our gardens. Every day the garden area gets larger and more vegetables are planted. There is an abundance of insects, but in spite of the bugs the garden is progressing nicely. The soil is gratifyingly fertile and things grow in much less time than the seed catalogues say. The leafy-type vegetables simply grow faster than the bugs can eat them, and the plants look good. But we are having trouble with ants and beetles and worms underground, which eat a good deal of the carrots, beets, and potato-type vegetables. There is no rain, of course, so that everything has to be watered, but this is not too arduous.

The well we are digging is not making much progress. The fellows dug down to a solid layer of rock and then had to stop digging until we could get two steel chisels. With them they managed to chop a small hole in the rock, and about three hundred gallons of water seep up through it every day. We won't have a good well, however, until we can crack this solid rock wide open.

I realize more and more as the days go by what a wonderful fellow Surin is. Without him this village would never have been started. He seems to be doing everything and be everywhere at the same time. He works as hard as anybody else and then gives more of his time to treating the sick and looking after everyone's problems. And for myself, instead of getting tired of his company I have come to appreciate it more and more every day. His wife, Lai, is a very fine cook and she has recently been making some delicious pineapple pies. Poor Lai, the day she first came to the village and saw that it was not yet a village at all she almost broke down and cried. I remember she said, "I am not asking you where we are going to stay, I am not asking you where we are going to sleep. I am asking you where I am going to stand." She soon settled down and became a most valuable member of our little community. She and Surin had been married for some time and knew a lot about the business of running a household.

I heard an interesting story today. Apparently the valley in which we have made our village is known locally as the Valley of the Lepers. It was given this name many years ago because some lepers used to live in it. And the local tradition has it that one day more lepers would return and make their home there. It is strange to think that we are fulfilling a local legendary prophecy.

Now that the weather is better and our village is reasonably established we are working on our roads. It is now possible to drive from the main road into our village, and we have repaired and reinforced all the wooden bridges across the streams.

We borrowed the use of some of the local working elephants to drag in the heavy logs used as the bridge spans; the planking was all sawed by hand from trees. This heavy sawing usually means that a few pair of crippled hands get too bruised to work and our labor force is temporarily cut down. We keep at the work, however, because the road and bridges are too important to neglect.

All the married men have left the dormitory building and moved into little houses on the hills surrounding the village. Every day we push our village into the jungle just a little bit more. Surin and his wife were the first couple to set up a home, and they were followed by Leah and her husband, Dao, then Gia and Suk, and Nahngsan and his wife. The village is no longer just a collection of buildings but is now a group of living family units. When I stop to think that these people were once social outcasts who felt that life had passed them by, I can't help feeling a little proud.

Though we had achieved no more than a sparsely inhabited clearing in the jungle, it seemed to Surin and me at the time that we had achieved a great deal, and we decided to set out and find new worlds to conquer. I feel now that maybe we should not have attempted to enlarge our project until Trinity Village itself was at least partly self-supporting. But we were inexperienced and headstrong real-estate developers, and there seemed no reason for not getting other villages going at the same time.

We had heard that in Chonburi Province, south of Bangkok, there was a village with an unusually high incidence of leprosy. There is a sort of leprosy grapevine system among patients throughout the country that relates such information. We decided to go down—a mere six hundred miles—and find out what we could do about it. Accordingly we packed a toothbrush and a change of clothes and set off.

I recorded our trip in my diary when we returned three weeks later.

December 16, 1955

Surin and I have just returned from our trip to Chonburi, Bangkok, and Chainot, and it really feels good to be home again, for that is how I think of Trinity Village. I seem to be becoming rather a weakling these days, as half of the time I am suffering from either a cold or diarrhea. Perhaps the climate and the local food at last are beginning to catch up with me. Anyway, it will be good not to have to travel for a while and to be able to stay in one place and relax.

Surin, his wife, and I left Trinity Village on Tuesday, November 29, by bus and stayed that night in Chiengmai. On Wednesday morning we left by train for Bangkok. I wanted to give Surin and Lai a vacation, as they have been working for no salary, and so I took them in a first-class compartment. I think they really enjoyed the trip. We arrived in Bangkok on Thursday morning and immediately found a bus leaving for Chonburi. I made a quick dash to buy some German sausages and then clambered on the bus. About noon we arrived in the village just outside Chonburi where Guee (an ex-McKean patient) lives. He had not yet received Surin's letter giving the day of our arrival, and so there was nothing ready for us to do that afternoon. We just relaxed on the beautiful ocean beach.

Word was soon spread that anyone with leprosy who wanted treatment should come and see us. On Friday a few people straggled in and we had seven patients diagnosed and taking treatment by the late afternoon. That evening two men came from the village and asked us to go with them to see a couple of patients who were too embarrassed to be seen in daylight. We followed them through some narrow alleys and over some rickety plank walks to some dwellings built out over the sea. In the first hut there was a boy of about eighteen with a terrible lepromatous face and in the middle of a reaction—a flare-up of worsened symptoms. He was set out by himself in the corner of the yard and he looked utterably miserable. We left DDS medicine for him and also for his sister, whom we found to be in an early stage of infection.

The next place we were taken to had a man who was an advanced case and hadn't been out of the building for eighteen years. Though his parents were caring for him he seemed more dead than alive.

From there we were taken to an outhouse behind some shops

under a pier where we found a girl of about twenty. Her parents had tried to treat her with some Chinese medicine which only made her deaf and didn't touch the leprosy. She had then been chased from her home and was now an outcast existing on scraps of food left for her by two local shopkeepers. She lived in complete misery and despair under the leaky planks of the pier. That night I couldn't sleep for thinking of what a horrible disease leprosy is.

On Saturday a continuous stream of patients came to the house of Guee, and we eventually placed twenty-five more under treatment, having turned away at least fifteen who did not have leprosy but other forms of skin disease. We had been told that most of the lepers in this area were suspicious of leprosy workers because they were afraid they would be taken off to the Phra Pa Daeng government colony near Bangkok. We were therefore surprised and unprepared to have so many come to visit us.

Before we left on Sunday we were able to treat four more patients bringing our total number of registered leprosy patients in that village to forty. In Bangkok we found that the King's birthday was being celebrated. Since I wanted to go to the Immigration Department to get an extension for my visa we had to wait for the holiday to end. We took in some Thai boxing and wandered around the city. When I got to the Immigration Department I was told that there would be no trouble whatsoever about my staying in Thailand for as long as I wished. Official word was also sent up to Chiengdao confirming this extension. We also went to the Ministry of Public Health and told them what we were trying to do. They assured us that they approved of it completely. We left Bangkok by the local train on Wednesday morning for Takli. The distance is only about a hundred and fifteen miles but it took us six and a half hours. At Takli we got on a bus and rode to Chainot and spent the night in a rickety old Chinese hotel overlooking the river. The next day we went by riverboat upstream to the village of Wat Sing, where we stayed in one of the smallest hotels I have ever seen. It had four tiny rooms and was upstairs over the local "dentist." While eating lunch there we became acquainted with two of the local businessmen and found them to be interested in our work. One of them sent us up in one of his huge lumber trucks to the village where Sawang, another ex-McKean patient, lives. The road was the worst in the world. Some places were a maze of oxcart ruts three or four feet deep, and other places were lakes several feet deep. The big four-wheel-drive vehicle made the five-mile journey in just over an hour and a half. We had heard so much about the high incidence of leprosy in this village that we had thought it would be a good place to start a village of our own. However, we decided to drop this idea, at least temporarily, after talking with Sawang. Nearly every family in the village had at least one member with leprosy and nobody seemed to object to it. Indeed there is so much leprosy that it is almost a leper village now. It is much better from our point of view to supply an established village like this with the medicine than to have to start a new village. We stayed in Wat Sing only one day and then on Friday returned to Chainot and then on by bus to Takli. There was no train that day to Chiengmai so we had to spend another day in Takli before catching the midnight slow to Chiengmai.

December 22, 1955

It is now almost Christmas but it certainly does not feel like it. Last night we had a little service and sang some Christmas carols for the dedication service of Dao and Leah's new house. It is the custom in Thailand for every new house or building to have a ceremony and feast, usually to protect the house from the spirits. Thai people who have become Christians have changed the traditional spirit-appeasing service into a dedication service to God. We were able therefore to sing "Silent Night" and other favorite carols and it did seem a little like Christmas. Apart from this, nothing very interesting has happened and our days are busy not with celebrations and holidays, but with the hard work of tending the gardens and clearing land for new houses. We are beginning to find that the work is getting easier, I think because nearly everyone including me has become hardened. I am very pleased to see that many of the leprosy patients have grown noticeably heavier and stronger. A few nights ago we had three new men come into the village and another man and his wife came yesterday. [These people had heard of our village through the leprosy grapevine, as we had never made any public announcement about our village and never needed to in the future.] A few nights after the three men arrived, one of them got up in the middle of the night and stole the clothing and money from the man sleeping next to him. Then he ran away. By the time the other men had awakened in the morning the thief had got on a bus to Chiengmai and disappeared. I find this very strange. The man was a very bad case of leprosy and I cannot imagine why he would want to run away from the shelter, treatment, and security of our village just for a few stolen *baht*. I am afraid he will live to regret his action.

I had more snake trouble last night. I was sitting in my fine new leaf-covered bathroom when a snake came sliding in to investigate my lantern just inches from my feet. He was not very big and he ignored me completely, but he worried me. I do not like getting caught with my pants down.

Two months passed during which I did not make any entries in my diary. During this time a number of important things happened and I recorded most of them on February 24.

February 24, 1956

There are now forty-one patients living in Trinity Village and I understand that four more families will move up here next week. There are seventeen houses in various stages of completion.

My own new wooden house is now almost ready. It stands on the top of a small hill in the center of the village and I shall have a beautiful view from it in all directions. We have managed to camouflage most of our glaring carpentry errors so far, and the house looks quite good.

Our gardens look nice, although the work on them has slackened off during the last month. It seems that nearly everyone prefers building houses to raising vegetables. I cannot say I blame them. We have now cleared a large area, though, and it no longer looks as if the jungle could grow in on us during the night.

Unfortunately now that we have more people we have more jealousy, hurt feelings, and petty squabbles to deal with. Gahmooen and others have been raising chickens but have no fences to pen them in. Pahn and others have been raising corn and other vegetables. Some chickens were seen eating the newly planted seeds. Later the same chickens dropped dead from poison after eating some seeds from the second planting. Nobody claims any further knowledge but some accusing looks are being cast. Nahngsan and Kumpayow came to blows over a disputed planting of a single row of pineapple shoots. Each claimed the land the row was on (a matter of about two feet) yet either could have expanded his land in other directions without restriction. It is difficult for me to find out the real reasons behind some of these squabbles because in good Oriental custom nobody ever gives the real reason for a quarrel. I only hope Surin will find out as much as possible and let me know if any of the quarrels seem to be becoming serious.

About a month ago I decided that I would like to take some pictures of opium poppy fields and opium processing. Leah, the Mao girl, agreed to take us to her home village and help me get the pictures I wanted. This sounded as if it would be a great experience, and so off we went. We started off by bus to Chiengmai and spent the night there in a small Chinese hotel. I bought a supply of bread for the approaching trip but found when I awoke that most of it had been eaten by rats. It was a poor way to begin but my spirits were high and I felt strong enough to tackle any obstacle. We caught the 6:30 A.M. train to Lampang, from where we took a bus over an impossible road to Jehom. I was ready to hike the distance to the next village but Surin suggested that we hire an oxcart instead. We did, and arrived in Jesorn at about eight in the evening. The village headman gave us a place to sleep on the floor of his hut. The next morning I still felt that I could tackle anything and we started off on the last leg of our journey. We decided to hire a man to carry our bedrolls and camera equipment, although I felt guilty about what I thought would be a needless expense. By noon I realized that a carrier was no luxury. The mountains got higher and the sun got hotter and my legs did not feel nearly so strong as they ought to. After lunch by the side of a little mountain stream I felt a little better and was able to take in the scenery once again. This feeling of strength left me again after another hour's climb in the hot sun and my senses were soon down to the level where I was conscious only of plodding along step by step.

About three o'clock in the afternoon we crossed a ridge and there was a Mao village nestling in the valley below us. At last I thought we had arrived but Leah informed us that this was not her village. Her village was over the next mountain. We climbed on. As we passed through the first village Leah greeted her friends and neighbors. I made a special effort to look fresh and unconcerned, but as soon as we got through the village I had to sit down and rest. Then we began the long steady climb of the next mountain. At first I was able to cover fifty or sixty steps without a rest but after a very short time I was resting after ten or twelve steps. Our carrier had disappeared ahead of us and Leah and a couple of Mao children she had met in the previous village ran on ahead. We finally hobbled to the top of the crest and there was Leah's Mao village below us. A mere cluster of ten crude wooden buildings with pigs and chickens and children scrabbling around in the dust, but it was the most welcome sight I had ever beheld. I think now that if the mountain had been ten feet higher I would never have made it. We were invited into one of the houses where most of the people seemed to have gathered to welcome us. The house was like all the other houses: it was built of crude wooden planks standing on end and covered with a roof of thatch. There were no windows and the door was about four feet high and kept closed all the time. There was a fire burning in the room but no chimney, so smoke was everywhere. The ceiling was coated with what seemed to be at least an inch of greasy black soot. Two of the Mao tribespeople sat smoking huge bamboo water-cooled pipes which gurgled loudly every time they inhaled.

A hot, smoky hut was no place for me to relax after my strenuous climb and so I begged to be excused and crawled out into the hot but somewhat cleaner air. After a while the villagers seemed to become aware of my problem and they showed Surin and me to an equally smoky, sooty hut where we could lie down and rest.

I am afraid I was not so observant as I ought to have been during my visit to Leah's village, because my main concern was with garnering enough strength for the return journey. Dead though I was, I could not help noticing what unusual people Mao are. Every so often they sounded a gong to frighten away evil spirits from the village. In fact everything they did was either to protect themselves from spirits or to appease them. The absence of windows and the closed doors in their houses were attributable to their fear of spirits. At night when we bedded down we were asked to point our heads in a certain direction so that the spirits would not be confused and angered. It must be terrible to spend one's life in complete and abject fear of thousands of evil spirits one supposes to be around him all the time.

I took my films of the opium cooking just before the sun set and some films of the opium fields the following morning. The steps in the collecting and cooking of opium are as follows: when the blossom loses its petals the bulbs of the blossoms are slit lightly five or six times. From these slits a sap runs out and collects in little balls which are scraped off the bulbs the following day. This sap is then carried back to the village where it is put into a pan of boiling water. When the sap has melted and mixed with the water the mixture is strained through a cloth which removes all the dirt and fibers. The mixture is then placed in another pan which is kept on the fire until the water evaporates, leaving only the pure opium ready for smoking. The entire process is very simple.

The return journey to Lampang was much easier. There we took the train to Bangkok as we were to go on to visit our leprosy work at Angsela near Chonburi. We found the patients in good spirits and soon registered another new group of patients, bringing our total there to ninety. One of the men in the village who had a daughter suffering from leprosy turned over the use of his house to our workers to live in and use as a clinic. The man was the caretaker of a wealthy man's beach house and was not using his home. Mungjai (another ex-McKean patient) is now living in Angsela carrying on our work, and Boonkrong and his wife will move down there from Chiengdao to take charge of the work in a week's time.

From Chonburi we returned to Bangkok and then up to Wat Sing outside of Chainot. We were able to get a ride from Wat Sing to our leprosy village where we found good progress being made. As there was very little we could do we decided to walk back to Wat Sing and not wait for the bus the next day. I reasoned that if we walked back we could return the same day to Takli and catch the late Chiengmai train. This proved to be a foolish move. I was, I suppose, worn out from my mountain climbing; anyway after walking across rice paddies in the blazing hot sun for several hours I began to feel that something was wrong. I staggered into Wat Sing and flopped down on a hotel bed, hoping that I would snap out of it in an hour or two. Instead I developed a fever of one hundred and three that lasted for eight days. Four of those days I stayed in the hotel room in Wat Sing, but I became so ill that I couldn't eat and Surin helped me to get to Manorom, another nearby village where the Overseas Mission Fellowship was building a hospital. There I stayed with Mr. and Mrs. Ferguson, and the OMF doctor, Dr. Chris Madox, took care of me and my heat exhaustion. After five days I was sufficiently improved to travel and Dr. Madox put me on the train to Chiengmai. Mr. and Mrs. Ferguson and Dr. Madox were all wonderfully kind to me and I shall always remember everything they did. I told them about our leprosy work. Dr. Madox and another OMF missionary, Barbara Morgan, told me that the OMF was getting many new workers in that area and that they intended to expand their own work in leprosy. I told Dr. Madox that it would be much better if the OMF and Barbara Morgan in particular could take over the work we were trying to do in that area. They agreed and I think they may. This would leave us with Trinity Village and the work we are doing in Chonburi. If this is not enough to occupy me I am sure I can soon find somewhere else to start something.

March 9, 1956

We now have about fifty-five patients plus eight small children living here. There do not seem to be too many crucial problems but we are certainly swamped with minor and irritating ones. I feel ready for a vacation.

I cannot believe that there is any other kind of work in which a person's emotions cover such a range in so short a period of time. One minute I am choked up and practically in tears, and then suddenly I am raging in anger at somebody. Somebody always wants to pick up all the choice garden vegetables before the others get a chance. Somebody else will not work because somebody else is not working. Everyone wants his house finished first but nobody wants to help anyone else.

We now have fifteen houses completed and others under construction—not including my own castle on the hill, which is still short of a roof because we have not sufficient money to buy any tiles. The patients work for the colony projects in the morning and for themselves in the afternoon. I guess we now have about ten times more land cleared than we had cleared three months ago. We are really beginning to look like a settlement.

In spite of all the irritations I am enjoying this experience. Something new is always happening to me. Two nights ago while I was reading by lamplight a chicken hawk came roaring in and crashed against the flimsy bamboo walls. Surin quickly hit it on the head and the neighbors had hawk curry for breakfast the next day. I do not know why in the world the crazy bird flew into our house.

My major complaint at the moment is the noise made by village roosters every night. I am sure we have two of the crowiest roosters in the world. They are not big or pretty but they sure can keep a fellow awake at night. It is strange, though; I do not think I have been anywhere in Asia where there have not been roosters crowing all night. It does not make any difference whether I am in the center of Bangkok or Hong Kong or Manila. There are always roosters crowing all through the night.

The weather is now beginning to get hot and I am beginning to wilt. I feel somewhat better after my illness but I have lost a lot of stamina, I seem to notice the heat much more quickly when the sun gets hot in the afternoons.

April 8, 1956

The hot season is on us once again and I cannot say I am too happy about it. During the afternoons the air gets so hot you can feel the pressure forcing in on you and drying up all body moisture, even inside. One hardly perspires. It is difficult to believe just how dry a tropical jungle can get. All the leaves dry up and fall from the trees eliminating the shade and making things worse. Nearly all small plants and bushes shrivel up and die. Whereas a few months ago there was an almost solid wall of vegetation surrounding the village, now there is a barren space for at least a hundred yards all around. Most of the trees are so large that they do not grow very close together. Therefore, when the leaves and underbrush disappear everything appears open and bare. The earth becomes like powder and a single person strolling along a trail will raise a cloud of dust. If you pick up a handful of dirt it powders off the hands like talcum. Fires are common and nearly everyone seems to feel that it is his duty to start a fire. Hunters like to burn off the undergrowth so that they can see the animals more readily. Some burn off areas to be used for crops or roads or houses. But about 90 per cent of the fires seem to be started merely because people enjoy starting them. The air becomes hazy with smoke and burns and smarts the eyes. The sun can barely be seen glowing weirdly through the haze. It is hard to realize that in only a few weeks when the rains begin again everything will once more turn to a solid screen of green.

We now have twenty-one houses completed here in the village and three more almost completed. I sometimes wonder if the people would not have been better off if they had gone slower on house building and spent more time on gardens and other productive projects. However, people who have never had a home cherish the thought of having their own dwelling even though it may only be a bamboo hut.

Last week I nearly had a fight with a cobra in my garden. As I was looking at our cabbages I suddenly heard a clatter from one of our sprinkling cans which had been overturned just behind my feet. I wheeled around in time to see the ugly black form of a six-foot cobra go sliding over the bank into the brush by the river. Apparently the snake had been sleeping under the water-can, enjoying the heat of the sun, and had been awakened by my stomping around. I was standing barely a foot or so from the can and I would have been an easy target if the snake had had any desire to strike me. I am afraid I will never be a hero where snakes are concerned.

We had news today from our Wat Sing and Chonburi works. Ahnon is working in Wat Sing still and says that he is enjoying himself. We want him to go to Chonburi but he keeps on asking us for a little more time at Wat Sing. He says he now has ninety-five patients. Boonkrong has one hundred and sixty-five in Chonburi, which brings our total number of patients to two hundred and sixty. However, the patients in the Wat Sing area are no longer really ours, as the OMF Mission has taken them over for us. Since the work has been going for only eight months I do not feel that these statistics are too bad.

There was an accident on the road to Chiengmai the other day. One of the buses turned over and several people were killed. I have often thought about the danger of these buses. They are so jammed with rice sacks and people that nobody can move a muscle. The coachwork of the buses is made in Thailand of wood and set on an imported chassis. These wooden frames collapse completely in an accident. Unfortunately the drivers are cocky but not too skillful. They are proficient only at brakes and horns. And if either of these gives out they are done for.

April 19, 1956

The weather is if anything hotter than before although we have had a small cooling shower off Chiengdao mountain once or twice this week. As a matter of fact one of these showers almost ruined us a couple of days ago. Bamboo and leaf houses are fairly durable for a while but hot seasons are hard on them. A gentle shower will cause everything to swell and tighten nicely again. But this last shower hit the bamboo house before the rain had given the structure an opportunity to swell and tighten. The wind was so strong we suddenly found ourselves with a flying roof, and Surin and Lai had to hold things together while I found a few nails and rope.

There seems to be a tremendous number and variety of bees and hornets flying around here trying to build nests. I have had to knock hornets' nests off my bed legs and suitcases and shoes and clothing. I have killed dozens and smashed many nests but still they keep buzzing around. I have been stung many times but fortunately the effects of the stings wore off fairly well in a few days and I am not too bothered.

I am trying to inspire a little more concern among the patients for colony equipment. For the most part they neglect equipment except when they want to use it. Nobody wants to be responsible for keeping things in repair. Also I find that they are not really interested in helping to form policy. When some question as to policy arises I try to have the patients voice their own ideas. They are quick to criticize after something has been settled but they hate to take any responsibility for deciding things in the first place.

May 13, 1956

I moved into my new house about three weeks ago and I found it much cooler. Of course it is raining nearly every day now so this helps to cool things. There is still a great deal of work left to do before the house is completed. Most of my spare time now is spent in trying to make windows and trim from teakwood. The patients saw the wood into boards for me and I pay them for their labor.

One of the amazing things to me about this country is the

tremendous waste. I am certain there is twice as much food thrown away as garbage here as in America. I have always looked on Americans as wasteful people, but they cannot hold a candle to the Thai. This same extravagant attitude affects their handling of money. They never save anything. It must be spent immediately. And sadly it is rarely spent on necessities. The average working man's salary runs to about five hundred *baht* a month. Of this he spends one hundred *baht* a month on cigarettes and about one hundred and fifty *baht* on lottery tickets or gambling. At least another fifty *baht* is spent on liquor or movies. This means that he lives on two hundred of his five hundred *baht*. If he saved three hundred *baht* a month instead of wasting it he would be a wealthy man in a few years. But it seems to make no difference how large a salary he receives, most of it is gone before the end of the month on things which are of no permanent value to him.

[In January of 1956 we had had a bountiful harvest of cabbage and I was delighted with our first salable surplus. Each villager typically took enough for only a meal or two; he felt that each share wasn't enough to sell but was more than he cared to eat. Thus, at least a hundred heads rotted away in our shed.

I gradually learned that the concept of budgeting was virtually unknown. A surplus and then a shortage was to be expected. After years of working with these people I'm convinced that learning to earn is not nearly so urgent a problem as learning to live on what they earn.]

Quite a large area has been cleared and prepared for pepper plants which we hope to set out this week. Everyone thinks he will make a fortune by raising peppers but I am not so confident. Many of the patients are buying banana plants and setting these in and also a few pineapple and other fruits. Eventually, I hope, ours will be a productive little area. Meantime it seems that for every plant we finally raise we lose a couple to the goats, a couple to the bullocks, a couple to buffaloes, a couple to insects, and a couple to the careless hoeing of the gardeners.

Although we are hardly ready for childbirth we picked up an expectant mother as a patient. She had been in the McKean Colony but when she became pregnant without being married she was told that she had to leave immediately. I do not exactly condone her actions but on the other hand I do not know of anybody who needs help more than she and so we have taken her in. There is no doubt that it must be pleasant for the McKean Colony to get rid of its moral problems, but sending them out the gate is no solution.

Last Sunday somebody killed a female gibbon in the jungle and brought back her baby to me. I immediately took possession of him and am now playing nursemaid. When I first got him he was so small he could not stand and seemed to feel that everyone was a gibbon just like him. No matter how or where I held him he would bite, expecting to find milk, and he got pretty disgusted when he didn't. We mixed some powdered milk and a little sugar and soon taught him to eat from a spoon. Now he practically works the spoon by himself. At first he cried terribly if no one held him tightly all the time. Now, though he still prefers to be held, he seems fairly comfortable on an old towel. He is a nuisance but a lot of fun. If he is on a bare floor he is clumsy and helpless but in a tree he is a picture of ease and comfort. The only trouble is that he would rather hang on to someone's neck or arm than on to the limb of a tree. The big gibbon is getting rather weary of the little fellow. I do not think the old fellow can ever remember seeing another gibbon and he has probably forgotten that he is a gibbon himself.

During the past few weeks the patients have killed a number of cobras when the snakes came after the chickens. I have not taken any part in this activity as I am still not particularly eager to be able to say I have killed a cobra. I feel I can live quite well without having this experience. We are again short of supplies. Our shipment of DDS from the Mission has not arrived yet so we shall have to buy some. Surin and I must go to Chonburi in another week and check on the work there before Boonkrong leaves for Bible School. We are also acutely short of money. I must pay Boonkrong's Bible tuition costs for him and as it is the time for planting crops I have to buy pepper plants and garlic. The taxes must also be paid this month. The number of our patients increases and the cost of rice to feed them is going up all the time. Expenses rise daily and contributions do not keep pace. If only we had just that little extra money. It would make all the difference as we could buy the important things without counting and worrying about every penny.

June 3, 1956

Surin and I made the trip down to Chonburi two weeks ago. We left here on a Monday morning and arrived in Chiengmai about noon. We caught the afternoon train to Bangkok, arriving Tuesday noon. For several hours we chased around the town trying to get some DDS and then took a bus to Chonburi and got there about suppertime. This was a new speed record for us but I cannot say I enjoy traveling at such a pace. I do not know why it is but I seem to have no stamina any more. When we arrived in Chonburi I felt completely exhausted and did nothing but lie on my bed for a few hours to recover. The new house that Boonkrong and the boys had moved into in Angsela was on the main street and had been built as a store originally. It was large and comfortable with fluorescent lights but it had no toilet. As I have been afflicted with diarrhea for weeks now, I did not like the idea of having to squat in somebody's back yard every once in a while, so Surin and I decided we would go to a small Thai hotel in Chonburi. The hotel had one toilet to accommodate guests in twenty rooms. Americans always think in terms of conveniences, I suppose, and the location of the toilets is one of our primary concerns.

Thai people seem to feel one can relieve himself anywhere. Even their best houses usually have inferior toilets and bathrooms.

Everything seemed to be progressing well at Chonburi so we did not stay long and left on Friday. There are over one hundred and eighty patients there now.

On Saturday morning we saw Boonkrong off to Khonkaen, where he would go to Bible School. We still could not get the DDS from the East Asiatic Company and so we had to go back to Chiengmai without it. We had stayed in Bangkok this time just long enough to make inquiries about DDS and arrange for it to be shipped up to us as soon as it arrived. I dislike the noise, heat, and confusion of the city more and more as time passes.

We are setting out our tung-oil trees and have set in over seven thousand pepper plants. The door to my bathroom has finally been finished.

The little gibbon is getting so spoiled that he demands to be carried all the time. If we set him down he protests so loudly that usually we pick him right up again. I am sure he has forgotten he is a gibbon and can climb trees.

A few weeks ago a couple of elephants were driven through our village and I took some pictures of them. Two days after I had taken the pictures one of the elephants killed his driver. The elephant had already been chained before the driver was killed and now everyone is worried that he will break his chains and go on a rampage. Most of the elephants in this district are owned by a man in the next village and that is where the driver was killed. This was the fifth man this elephant had killed. No one will destroy an elephant in this country, however, if he can avoid it. When the beast finally quiets down a little he is given a new driver and sent off to work again. The people in our village have made some long spears which they claim will ward off an elephant in case a difficult one comes through here. I am afraid I have little confidence in a spear. I feel more secure in my wooden house although I suppose that if the elephant wanted to, he could walk straight through it. If there is one thing I would rather meet less than a king cobra it is a crazed elephant.

June 26, 1956

Last week Surin and I went down to the Leprosy Conference at McKean Colony timed for Dr. Robert Cochrane's visit to Thailand. The medical lectures were a good review for me, although a lot of the material concerning smears and slides was of little benefit to us as we have no microscope.

My little gibbon is getting stronger and more spoiled every day. I do like him in spite of his naughtiness. He is such good company and helps me to get out of myself. The pepper fields are beginning to look very good and the tung-oil trees are growing well. Although we have a lot of plants under cultivation, when I look around the area I see vast tracts of land that we have not even touched. We are planning to plant asparagus, beans, and garlic soon. There is so much more work to be done here that I sometimes wonder if we'll ever get it really well developed. It takes so much effort for these poor leprosy patients to hack away at the jungle with their broken and deformed hands that I hesitate to push them too far. I do not know very much about using agricultural machinery but I am sure that a tractor with some kind of implement behind it could do the clearing in a few days.

July 12, 1956

At last we got a check for $600 from the First Lutheran Church. This had been promised many months ago and I was beginning to despair of ever receiving it. It could not have come at a more useful time. It has enabled us to buy the pineapple plants and garlic and bean seeds. I have also been able to pay for the lumber that the men have sawed for me and to make loans to the villagers so that they can buy pigs, chickens, and seeds. Also I have at last been able to buy two chairs for the house. For eleven months we have not had a chair of any kind and now when I sit down on my wooden chair I feel as if I am a civilized man again. This constant worrying about money makes me think that I am becoming much too materialistic. In the past I hardly cared if I had money or not. But having been without it for so long and needing it for so many different purposes, I find myself thinking about money now far more than I ought to.

For the past week or so we have had a crew of men working to build or repair the bridges on our private road. The men decided to build the bridges out of teak logs as these would be strong and would last almost forever. They cut down some splendid trees and cut the logs into suitable lengths. Then they split the logs down the center and made planks ready to lay across the rivers and streams. If we had had to buy all that teak it would have been cheaper to build steel bridges instead. We did not buy it, however; we just borrowed it for a while from the nearby jungle. Nobody really owns these teak trees but the Thai government prohibits anyone from cutting them without special permit. Of course the jungle people in the area use them all the time and nobody ever seems to complain, so when we need something we just go in and help ourselves and hope for the best. The most remarkable thing about our bridges is the way which the crippled lepers struggled and strained to get the logs into place. When I watch these scrawny little guys with their crippled hands and bad feet swinging into a job that few well people would attempt, I am really awed. It is a remarkable sight to see men without fingers grab up a two-man saw and bring down a tree. When they cut down a tree they loop a rope around one end of it and then about a dozen fellows painfully drag the log to the bridge site. Their stump feet sometimes let them down and they stumble and slide through mud and over rocks as if they were drunk. They bellow and grunt at the tops of their lungs but finally get themselves where they want to go.

I am doing badly on my adjustment to scorpions here. We have now killed seven scorpions in my new house since we moved in about three months ago. Nobody has been stung yet but it is only a matter of time. The scorpions are not deadly poisonous, which is something to be grateful for, but their stings are painfully unpleasant.

The other day we had more elephant trouble. Three elephants trampled through several of the patients' rice fields and did a lot of damage. Fortunately they were working elephants, not wild ones, and we were able to trace the owner and collect damages. What happens is that at night the elephant drivers usually let the elephants wander in the jungle to feed. These elephants had traveled over five miles from their resting place. Perhaps our village is getting a jungle reputation for quality produce.

Last week a hunter from a nearby village was struck and killed by a king cobra. He was with a party of hunters and all ran away when they saw the snake. The snake gave chase and struck the last man in the middle of his back. The king cobra is one of the few snakes that will deliberately attack a man and it attacks not so much out of fear as out of sheer bad temper and aggressiveness. Most other snakes will get out of your way as soon as they feel you coming but the cobra is quite content to lie in wait and strike without provocation.

July 18, 1956

I am afraid I have had some bad news. For the last few weeks I have been getting more and more excited because it was arranged that my parents would come out for a few weeks' visit. Now I have received a letter from them saying that my father's kidney started hemorrhaging on the train from Albert Lea to San Francisco and that they had had to cancel their trip. I have been dreaming and planning how wonderful it would be to have the folks visit here and of all the places and things I would show them. But now my plans must be completely changed. I do not know exactly how seriously ill my father is but I think I shall have to fly home as soon as they can send me money for the ticket. When everything is all right at home it is not too bad to be stranded out here without money even to get home on. But when something like this happens I feel so helpless. There is nothing I can do but wait until somebody sends me some money. I do not think I shall ever come out here again unless I have funds of my own on hand. I do not yet know when I leave for home but it should be fairly soon. On my way to Bangkok to pick up a plane I shall go over to Chonburi for a few days to make sure that everything is going on well. The boys write that we now have two hundred and thirty-one patients there. In a sense I am possibly glad that something has happened to make me leave earlier than I expected. Ever since I got laid out by the sun last February I have been prone to headaches and even if I am out-side for a short time I return to my house completely exhausted with an extremely severe headache. Consequently I have not been able to do much physical work and this in itself has made me even softer physically. I think I need a period of rest, good food, and good living to recuperate for a while. As the days go by I seem to feel weaker and weaker and more and more listless. I try to show as keen an interest in everything going on around me as before but often it is almost too much effort to walk around the village to find out what is going on. I do not think I can have caught any tropical disease because I have no fever or anything like that. It is just this permanent weakness and listlessness that worries me. And of course the intermittent diarrhea, but all foreigners seem to suffer from that for at least several years when they come to the East, particularly if they live in the jungle. It is not so bad for people who live in Bangkok in modern houses with air-conditioning, refrigerators, and boiled water. They can buy all their food from stores or the PX and generally live in very much the same way as they live at home. But when you are deep in the jungle and living the same kind of life as the villagers, you are more exposed to the illnesses that they pick up. They have lived this way all their lives and have of course a considerable natural immunity. I have developed a fair immunity to most things, though it's not what it would have been had I been born here.

At the moment our gardens and crops look rather neglected. The rains cause the weeds to grow so fast that it is almost impossible to keep the fields clear. Almost as soon as people finish hoeing the field the first part of it is overgrown with weeds again. Not all our patients kill themselves with hard work, though there are some who work all the time and are always trying to find something else to do. One man has expanded his chicken flock from nine to more than a hundred, and he has increased the number of pigs from two to five. He also has pineapple, corn, and pepper fields growing. Another man has done absolutely nothing and yet he is a better physical specimen than the hard-working man. It is because of such differences in attitude that I am convinced my policy of helping those who help themselves is right. If we gave exactly the same amount of help to everyone regardless of what he did to improve his life, then the villagers could justly feel there was no real point in doing well. These people must be given an incentive. They must also be rewarded in some way when they show the right spirit.

July 20, 1956

I have received the money for my passage home and started packing my bag. This evening we had a colony meeting and tried to lay plans and policies for the time of my absence. On Thursday morning I gathered up my things, folded my cot, and killed three more scorpions that apparently wanted to come with me. Two of them were in my shoe and the other in my bag. Some of the patients said good-by to me in the village but a large number of them walked out to the road to see me off. The little gibbon also came to the road and tried his best to get on the bus. We stopped at Chiengdao briefly to check out at the police office and then spent a day in Chiengmai making arrangements with the post office and the bank for Surin to have the authority to handle all colony business. We went by train to Bangkok, arriving Saturday noon. Surin and I went immediately to a travel agent to see about my airplane accommodations to America. We had not had time to clean up after our hot dirty train ride so we made a fine impression. The travel people appeared not to mind. On Saturday afternoon Surin and I went to Chonburi by bus and stayed over night in the usual hotel. On Sunday we looked up Mungjai and Ahnon and tried to put all the affairs of the Chonburi work in order before returning to Bangkok on Sunday night. I had not felt at all well for the past few days and on Monday I felt so bad that I had to cancel my reservation and make a new arrangement and leave the following day. I could just not bring myself to get out of bed and go to the airport. Two days later I felt stronger and I was able to get to the airport and leave for America on a KLM plane. I spent most of the journey sleeping. I believe I slept more on that plane than all the other passengers put together. When we arrived in Seattle I was able to wake up and take an interest again. After all I was home in America again and would soon be in Minnesota.

Chapter 5

A year in America passed by very quickly. The first several months were largely spent in visiting my father in hospitals and in catching up on eating nearly forgotten favorite American foods.

As my father's condition gradually improved, I began to prepare for a return to Thailand. I spoke to all groups who invited me and I showed my films on leprosy. Gradually a reserve of money began to accumulate from the various donations and I began to entertain thoughts of being able to secure a jeep truck to take back with me. An Albert Lea merchant, Holger Knudson, donated money to purchase an irrigation pump and plastic hose for the village and my spirits soared once again.

Dr. Buker had also visited with me and had diagnosed and prescribed treatment for my amoebic dysentery now well established. His treatment raised my spirits considerably as I began to feel full of strength once again.

When it became apparent that I probably couldn't quite swing the jeep deal by my own efforts, my good friends from the men's group of Trinity Church once more came to the rescue and helped raise an additional thousand dollars. How delighted I was.

I made arrangements to sail on August of 1957 to return once again to my friends in Thailand. Just a few days before I was ready to leave, a young high school graduate, Bob Mortenson, asked to accompany me and spend the winter there before going on to his studies in college. It was thus with a happy heart that I started a trip for the third time for Thailand.

Bob and I planned to drive by jeep to the coast where we would board a Norwegian freighter for the Orient. Our brand-new jeep threw a rod when we had gone no farther than Sidney, Nebraska, however, and our cushion of time was consumed waiting for the repairs. Bob and I drove frantically day and night and reached the San Francisco pier just in time for loading the pump and the jeep. In our haste the engine never got properly adjusted and remained forever something of a lemon.

My feelings at returning once again to the familiar Asian scenes are expressed in my diary accounts of that time.

September 15, 1957

Well, I am back in Thailand staying at my old favorite, the Railway Hotel, in Bangkok. It seems as if I have never been away. Everything here is as it was before. Tuesday evening we arrived at the mouth of the river south of Bangkok and anchored there until daylight before going upriver to the piers. At about seven-thirty on Wednesday morning we pulled up to a pier and there were Surin and his brother waiting for us. It was good to see them again.

The immigration and customs officials were very helpful and all our small baggage was passed without inspection or duty. The customs will hold the .22 rifle, however, until we get our permit. This should be no problem as we shall get the permit easily in Chiengdao and we can then send for the rifle. The jeep will be cleared in another day or so.

As soon as we cleared customs we loaded everything into a taxi and moved to the Railway Hotel, where we have stayed ever since. I am really happy to see Surin again. He is his usual wonderful self and I enjoy talking to him so very much. We have been out on the town tasting again many favorite dishes. Yesterday noon while shopping for a coat for Surin we stopped in at a very pleasant Chinese restaurant for dinner. The food there was unusually good—and plentiful. Boys brought trays with a variety of choice Chinese dishes on them and then wandered among the tables allowing anyone to help himself to any dish he wanted. When we finished eating they simply counted the empty dishes on the table and charged us accordingly. I must have eaten at least twelve different kinds of food. This afternoon I think we shall go to see the boxing again. They have some special championship bouts today between the Thai and Japanese. This of course will be international-style boxing, not Thai style.

September 29, 1957

I am back in Trinity Village. I have been so busy that I have had little time to write in this diary. Now, however, on this peaceful afternoon I am going to record some of the incidents of the last two weeks. We got our jeep through customs on Monday afternoon September 16 and had to leave a deposit of $625. We got a refund later of a little over $100, so the total duty and clearance fees for everything came to slightly more than $500. This was not too bad at all.

On Monday evening an army general, Sarit Thanarat, took over the government and forced the old prime minister and the police chief to leave the country. There were soldiers and tanks and equipment all over the place but everything was very quiet and not a single shot was fired. Things were so peaceful that it was not until Surin turned on the radio and bought a newspaper that we heard what had happened. And yet our hotel was in the heart of Bangkok located over the railroad station. Everything, particularly business, went on as usual. I do not think this kind of *coup d'état* will make much difference to the official government policy.

On Tuesday morning we drove to Chonburi. We were stopped by army checkpoints several times on the way and even had to take a detour of an extra thirty miles because the main bridge to Chonburi was blocked to prevent troops from the south coming up and retaking the capital. We visited our main clinic in Angsela and talked to a few old patients and then returned to Chonburi to rent rooms for the night. On Wednesday morning we drove down to a location about forty miles south of Chonburi where Boonkrong felt we might start a village. We talked to an ex-McKean patient who worked at a new plantation there, and then returned to Angsela. We then went back to Bangkok the same afternoon and took the jeep to the Willys dealer to have it checked over. On Thursday morning we collected the refund from the customs and packed our bags all ready to go as soon as we could pick up the jeep. We got the jeep and left Bangkok at about two-thirty in the afternoon. The first hundred miles out of Bangkok were asphalted so we coasted fairly fast. We were heavily loaded with the equipment and bags, Surin and his brother Charn, and Ahnon and Sohng, so we did not try to push too fast. To the north of Lopburi it began getting dark and the good road ended. Then it began to rain and visibility was soon poor. We bumped and slithered along until we came to Takli, where we turned off hoping to stop for the night. The two small hotels were full, however, so there was nothing to do but pile back into the jeep and slosh off to Chainot. The roads were now soupy from the downpour and it was no fun trying to miss the endless chain of potholes. Every few hundred yards we had to squirm over a temporary narrow bridge which crossed one of the many irrigation canals recently dug to connect with the new dam. Chainot was dismal and damp. It was our proposed resting place, however, so it took on a very welcoming appearance. But here, too, the hotels were full and we were forced once again to drive off into the rain in search of accommodation farther along. The road to Nakornsawan was a terrible maze of potholes and mud and bridges and never seemed to end. It was eleven o'clock before we finally arrived and found a small hotel with room for us. The bed was hard and the rooms were noisy. I slept fine.

On Friday morning we started out again and found the roads continuously bad although passable. We ate lunch in Tak and then took off again for the stretch through the mountains. Actually the mountain driving was the best we had had so far, since there was so little traffic and the road was not rutted. Just before dark, when we were almost out of the mountains on to the Chiengmai plain, we were delayed by a bus that had slipped off one of the small temporary bridges and blocked the way. We were fortunate again, however, because the bus had been stuck for several hours and was almost out by the time we got there. We finally arrived in Chiengmai at about eight-thirty and settled down for the night in the Bungalow hotel.

On Saturday we bought a few groceries in the market and then drove up to Trinity Village. The road to our village was in the process of being remade by our patients and it had been filled in with soft new earth which the rain had turned into a sea of mud. About halfway in we got caught in a slight dip and were soon stuck fast. The tailgate of the jeep was level with the road at the back and so we simply slid everything out of the truck and onto the road. We had quite a few of the patients on hand to help now and so we lifted the jeep out of the mud. The equipment we carried into the village on an oxcart.

It was wonderful to see the patients and the village again. It was the same and yet different. There were banana and papaya trees all over the area all heavily laden with fruit. The patients' houses were more solidly built now and the pigpens and the chicken houses actually looked like something intended to keep animals in. Surin has a new house, a two-story affair with a place to park the jeep under one room. Lai and Leah had scrubbed my house clean and made the bed already for me to move in. It was a warm homecoming.

On Sunday we had the usual church service and Boonkrong preached. Boonkrong was up for a week's vacation. Bob accompanied the hymns on his trumpet and everything went fine. On Monday we went down to Mae Tang to see the immigration officials. Bob was given an extension and the officers said the immigration stamp put in my passport in Bangkok entitled me to remain in Thailand as long as I wanted to. We then went to Chiengmai for some supplies. On our return to the village we started painting my house. We had bought the paint in Chiengmai and been told by the Chinese merchant that it was a light green. On the house, however, it was the ugliest dark green I had ever seen. I was glad to get the insect screens painted any color at all so long as it put an end to their rusting, but I didn't like such a dark, dismal color on my house.

We fixed up the pump and though it works well I doubt if it will do all I was hoping it would do. We also gave the loom we had been given by friends in Binghamton, New York, to a woman to practice on; she seems to be doing fine. A couple of nights ago we had a general meeting and now I am back where I was a year ago. The charm of my return has worn off by now and I am once again confronted with the petty problems of greed and jealousy. There is nothing very serious going on and I suppose it is good to get my feet on the ground again and realize just what I am here for. After all I have not come for a holiday.

It seems that we are engaged in a struggle with a family of rats. It will be interesting to see who eventually controls my house—they or I. My dresser seems to be their special target and a battle seems to be shaping up for control of this strategic position. I suppose that rats are an improvement on snakes which came into my bamboo house, but frankly I could do without either.

This morning Surin nearly drowned and I am still shaking from the experience. We had gone deep into the jungle to the north looking for more of the large bamboo which is so ideal for building. As our fellows were completing the task of carrying out the bamboo and lashing it together to float downstream, we decided to return to our village by way of the river instead of the circuitous jungle trail. Though the river was at flood crest, raging over submerged trees and stumps, we still felt it was easier than the trail. We began to make our way trying to keep to the shallow weak side of the current.

At one point the current grabbed at us and Bob started swimming downstream. Surin also began to swim but suddenly found his foot caught in the crotch of a submerged tree. The force of the raging water prevented his backing up and the rolling tree pulled his head down under water. I frantically threw one arm around his chest. As the current tore at me I lunged desperately and caught an overhanging root with my free hand. Because I am taller and heavier I had a little more leverage against the stream and was able to hold on to Surin. Slowly his head inched upward until his face lifted above water and we could struggle to free his foot. Somehow we both managed to force our way to the riverbank. Drenched and shaking with exhaustion and fear we sat down and looked at each other. Fortunately Surin had not swallowed too much water but he was badly shaken. We must have sat there quite silently for at least half an hour until Surin looked up and gave me a shy smile. I grinned and we got up and went on our way.

October 27, 1957

The past month has been interesting but nothing spectacular has happened. Bob seems to have adjusted to things and is beginning to enjoy life a little. For a few weeks he had trouble with his stomach and his eyes and could not take much part in our daily routine. But he is coming along better now. We seem to have temporarily solved most of the colony problems and are making good progress again. I think the fact that I brought back a car and a pump made the patients think for a while that a golden age was just about to begin in which they would not have to do anything but sit back and hold out their hands. But now they are realizing the true situation and are working wonderfully again.

We suffered a serious loss when five of our largest pigs died one day from an unknown cause; otherwise things have been going well and there have been few setbacks. We have a good-sized field already planted with garlic and covered with straw and are working to plant about three times as much in adjoining fields. We are also planting peanuts and cabbage in large quantities. Our vegetable gardens are again situated on the riverbanks and look bigger and better every day. Part of the riverbank is used as colony land and part is used privately but nearly all of it is being used by us now. Our water wheels have not been completed yet this year but they should be ready soon. We used the pump to soak everything once and plan to use it again tomorrow. It works fine except it will not pump water up to my house, because my house is rather higher than I had thought.

We have really been giving the jeep a workout. We have been hauling in straw for the garlic and hauling in garlic and peanut seed. We have hauled in all sorts of supplies and taken groups of patients whenever we go anywhere. The roads have been miserable and we have been stuck more often than I care to remember. The little car has held up well except that it has developed a tendency to shimmy. Interestingly, the car has added to our prestige in the area. We are now looked up to far more than before and our patients are more proud also. Three times a week Bob and I have been driving in to Chiengdao to teach English to the government and police officials. They really seem to appreciate this and I enjoy teaching them. It makes a pleasant change. Bob has been working with the more advanced and I have been helping the beginners. We are now of course on the friendliest of terms with all the students and are really getting to know them.

The other day we took some movies and slides of a couple of the elephants working near here. For the past week or so the elephants have been hauling out logs from all over the jungle around our village. At night we frequently hear them trumpeting. We photographed a pair of elephants, a mother and her baby. I guess the baby stood about four feet tall but it will nurse from its mother for at least another year. The little fellow was as ornery as could be and had already developed a first-rate kick. Once he charged us and I felt sure he was going to wreck the camera, but he stopped just short of us. I suppose a baby elephant gets cocky because it knows its mother will finish any trouble that it starts. I would like to have a little fellow like this for my own.

We seem to have discouraged a couple of the smaller rats in our house but the biggest ones stay on. One of them is just too clever for me. We set four traps touching one another so that a square of space was left in the center. We put a banana into this space. The rat has now taken two bananas without even springing one of the traps. He must have a featherlike touch when he wants to; ordinarily, when he runs across the rafters he sounds like an elephant. We have also killed a few scorpions and a poisonous centipede in the house. The Carlsons have given me a little kitten which I hope will develop into a rat killer. So far the kitten is the only one who gets a good night's sleep. The rat is not the slightest bit bothered by it.

November 29, 1957

The biggest news this past month is the tremendous victory we finally won over the rats. For many weeks the rats would wake us up at night with the noise of their gnawing and we would drowsily pick up our flashlights and knives and go after them. We would come close sometimes and think we almost had one, but he would get away and be back to gnawing almost before we could get back into bed. It was the most discouraging sort of life. Then one night about two o'clock I heard the usual noise and set out in pursuit. Bob got up when I sounded the alarm, and we cornered the rat in the kitchen. We must have looked ridiculous chasing around the room, flailing away with our big jungle knives, and trying to keep the rat in the beam of our flashlights. It is a wonder we didn't cut each other's legs off. Suddenly the rat made a dash up the wall and I hit it twice with the knife. Just as I had started to shout in triumph I saw to my horror the bloody body of the rat topple off the wall and fall into our big pail of freshly boiled drinking water. We were rather short of water the next day but the victory was really worth the sacrifice.

I am spending what free time I have studying Thai. It seems terribly difficult to find enough time to study for more than an hour a day. That is hardly enough time to really get the language but I do seem to be improving slowly. Other things in the colony are coming along well, though not spectacularly so. The first garlic seed we used failed to come up at all and so we had to reseed. We are having reasonable success with the new seed. One of the water wheels is now completed and two others are being constructed. We are hoping they will provide all the water we need for everything except the pineapples, but we shall have to continue to use the pump to water the pineapples on the hill-sides. The little engine in the pump continues to work perfectly. The immediate garden project is raising peanuts, and our main difficulty is that the garden is so terribly dry and hard that unless we soak it for hours it is almost impossible to work. We have broken the blades of about six heavy-duty chopping hoes. It is hard to believe that only two months ago everything was flooded and the soil a muddy mess.

The weather is now getting quite chilly at night and sleeping is wonderful. We have given every patient a blanket but these blankets are not too good and will be pretty thin in a year's time.

They cost only a dollar a piece: we had no more money to spend.

A couple of weeks ago we went to Chiengmai for the Loi Kratong (Festival of Lights) holiday. We have been having a little trouble with the jeep shimmying and the first garage we went to could not correct it. We decided to go a day early for the celebrations so that we could take the car to another garage which everyone recommended highly. On the evening of Loi Kratong we went to the garage intending to pick up the repaired jeep. When we walked into the place we saw a most distressing sight. The right-hand door was off the car and mechanics were swarming all over it pounding out dents. Apparently the owner of the place had taken the jeep out for a trial run and smashed the right front side of it into the overhanging spare tire of an oncoming Japanese jeep. Our jeep had ripped the tire off the Japanese one but an awful mess had been made of our cab. The right side of the cab was pushed one inch farther back than the left side. The manager was very sorry, of course, and has done everything possible to correct things. The men working on the body have done a surprisingly good job so that it now looks as good as new. Strangely enough it does not shimmy either so perhaps the knock has done it good. I think we shall probably gain by the whole affair as the garage owner is now very friendly toward us. [Later we discovered the cab leaked during heavy rains and we never could remedy that completely.]

My biggest problem at the village at the moment is my old gibbon. He seems to be determined to become a crooner and wails and howls all day long. A gibbon howl is terribly penetrating and becomes exasperating after a while. He is disrupting the peace of the colony, to say nothing of my afternoon naps. When we throw stones to make him stop he simply dodges them or catches them and keeps on with his singing. I am afraid I shall have to get rid of him because he is getting to be a nuisance and I can think of no way to stop this noise.

January 14, 1958

It has been ages since I last wrote in this book, so I am going to have trouble remembering everything in detail. Most of the time up to Christmas was occupied with routine work. I have tried to spend as much time as possible studying Thai but have invariably ended up with only an hour or so a day.

We had a pleasant Christmas. A good number of our villagers have come to us from various mission leprosy projects and are Christians and celebrate Christmas even though most Thai people regard Christmas as just another day. The patients decorated the colony with colored paper lanterns which flickered prettily at night and even managed to look gay during the day. The day before Christmas the Nai Amphur (the district officer) and all the local government officials piled into a jeep and drove out to see us. They had heard the day before that we had just got an old refrigerator and so for Christmas they brought us a can of refrigerator kerosene, a case of pop, a can of Ovaltine, some canned milk, and crackers and oranges. The refrigerator had been abandoned by the Baptist missionaries in Chiengmai. For about $50's worth of repair work we got it to work fairly well during the cold season. It couldn't cope with the hot-season temperatures no matter what we did, however. Our visitors were all good Buddhists and yet they wanted to wish us a merry Christmas. We had become quite good friends during our English classes, of course, but even so I thought it was very nice of them to come to see us.

A rather strange coincidence took place while they were all here. Some outside people exploded a bomb in the river to kill fish. This is illegal, of course, and as we all plainly heard the bomb go off, I asked the Nai Amphur how we could stop it. They decided to arrest the fellows on the spot and dashed off into the jungle to catch them. You can imagine how surprised the culprits were to find themselves suddenly surrounded by all the police and government officials of the area. After a lecture the Nai Amphur let the men go in honor of Christmas Day.

On Christmas Eve we had a service and then sat around and ate cookies and drank tea. The little kids put on a concert and they took turns leading the children's songs they knew. They were very cute. On Christmas morning we had another service and then Bob and I went to Chiengmai for Christmas supper at the Overseas Missionary Fellowship house. There we had a fine feast of turkey with all the trimmings. The day after Christmas Orville Carlson and two young OMF missionaries came up with us to the village and preached at our main service and stayed to enjoy our colony Christmas feast of rice and curry.

On December 27 we left Chiengmai for a visit to our Chonburi work. The roads were better than they were last September but they were still rough and dusty. We stopped overnight at Nakornsawan and arrived in Bangkok on the afternoon of the second day. The jeep had taken quite a pounding and had begun to shimmy again during the last few miles and so we stayed on in Bangkok to have a new shimmy bar put in before going on to Chonburi. We didn't do very much in Bangkok except go to one or two Thai boxing matches and look around a bit. We also got the rifle from customs. We had the permit and everything ready, I thought, but I still had to sign at least a dozen more papers and collect forty-two official signatures before I could get the rifle out. I find Thailand has just a little bit of red tape also.

When we got to Chonburi, Surin, Bob and I stayed in a cabin on the beach. This was pleasant. After we had finished our work for the day we were able to swim in the sea. We drove out to many villages to see patients and looked over land where we hoped eventually to build another village. Unfortunately we saw no land which seemed particularly suitable. I took movies of Boonkrong and the fellows in one small rural village as he gave out medicine. We talked to Dan Cobb, the Baptist missionary in Chonburi, and he was warmly cordial. Chonburi has been designated as a Baptist area by the mission boards in Thailand, but Dan said the Baptists had no plans to do leprosy work yet and that we were welcome. I don't feel we shall have any trouble working with him. If the other Baptists are as nice, it will be a pleasure cooperating with them.

Surin and Boonkrong both knew some old patients in the Rajburi area of Thailand who say there are many lepers there and no work of any kind to help them. We are now seriously thinking about beginning a new work there. I think we shall send Simoi in another month or so to look over the area, and then we can go ourselves for a better look later on.

We finished our visit to the Chonburi work with a check of some patients in Paknam and then drove to Bangkok on Saturday afternoon. Having no plans for Saturday evening we decided to go somewhere where we could wear our white coats. We ended up in a place called Hoi Thien Lao. This was considered one of the best Chinese restaurants and night spots in Bangkok. It has several floors of private, special, or public dining rooms and a night club on the roof. When I was first in Bangkok in 1952 I went there with a couple of fellows for a Chinese meal. On this occasion we had the famous Peking duck. I had heard of Peking duck many many times in the past, but I had never had it before —even when I was in Peking. It is strange that I have had to wait twelve years to try it. It is truly delicious.

After the meal we felt like taking a look at the night club and giving Bob a chance to hear what kind of orchestra they had. We had no plans of staying long. But when the music started and the lights turned low and the couples began to dance it looked inviting. We began to dance with some of the attractive hostesses. Before I knew what I had done I had danced for three hours, mostly with the same girl. She couldn't speak a word of English. I wouldn't have believed I knew enough Thai to talk to anyone for three hours, but there I was chatting away like wild. I think this must be the finest way to learn a foreign language. I had a thoroughly enjoyable time until the bill arrived. It was a terrible shock, particularly to me as I was innocent of the fact that the girl's time is worth three dollars an hour and the 7-Up we had been drinking cost fifty cents a bottle. I came down from the clouds in a hurry—wiser and also refreshed by the diversion.

February 21, 1958

In one week from today we shall leave for Bangkok to send Bob on his way home. The time certainly passes swiftly. During the past few weeks we have been trying to show Bob everything that he might yet care to see. We went to the temple overlooking Chiengmai and also stopped at the waterfall there. We went to see the silk-weaving industries at Lampoon and also the shops run by the two Miss Thailand contest winners of past years. Bob has had no strong wish to visit a tribal village or to see the Burma border or the other usual things, so our sightseeing has been easily accomplished.

The last two months in the village have been largely taken up by building new houses and extending and improving our roads. The garlic and peanuts were planted a while ago and the water wheels provide the necessary water. We can only wait and see how well they produce. This sort of temporary lull in our farming has been a good time to build. We are extending a road along the bridge to the south which when completed will make a complete circle around our pineapple fields and orange groves. But the work is slow as a lot of big stumps have to be removed by hand or burned out. We have also been digging a new well for the south neighborhood and this is now almost complete.

During the last two trips to town we ordered five thousand new pineapple shoots to be set in during the rainy season. We shall also have about five hundred new shoots from our own plants. This means that by the end of the year we should have well over ten thousand plants in fields. We also bought two hundred pomelo (a citrus fruit about the size of grapefruit but sweeter) seedlings from the government experimental station at Mae Jo which we shall set in during the rainy season. We are tentatively planning to buy five hundred or more orange-tree seedlings from Bangkok and then maybe set in a thousand or two coffee trees. We have reached the point where a lot of the preliminary work in the village is complete and we can begin to work in earnest to develop our permanent orchards.

Several weeks ago we were invited to take part in the thanksgiving services and feasts at the Chiengdao Christian Church. We were all happy finally to be invited to join with them. Although we have been here for three years we have never had anybody from the Chiengdao church contact us. We had got the impression that no Christians existed in this area and were therefore happy to meet a few. The following Sunday we invited a group of them to worship with us and asked their pastor to preach.

The jungle hasn't seemed the same to me since we have so many more people and guns. We never see any gibbons or monkeys any more. Several of our fellows have become skilled in the manufacture of muzzle-loading muskets made from a section of pipe and a few odds and ends. When the teakwood stocks are carved and polished they make beautiful weapons. These muskets are fired by a common paper powder cap which ignites the home-made black powder about the way Daniel Boone's musket worked with a flint spark. If the powder load is not so powerful that it bursts the barrel the musket is fairly reliable, at least during the dry season. Rainy-season moisture makes them erratic. Of course you can also load them with all kinds of slugs and scraps which will produce a result like being hit with shrapnel.

I can still hear the monkeys and gibbons screaming playfully on the other side of the ridge but can't get close enough to see them. The other night we were kept awake for several hours listening to two deer calling to each other. The snake population doesn't seem to have diminished any, and we have frequent visitors. Once during the middle of Twee's Sunday sermon a large snake slithered by the church in search of a few chickens and the sermon was temporarily interrupted while two of our fellows calmly got up, killed the snake, and then just as calmly returned to their seats. Last night a leopard came into our colony chicken pen and carried off a big fat turkey. By the time our watchman could get out of bed and into his shoes the cat had disappeared with the turkey. We haven't been bothered like that for almost two years now. I hope our fellows can hunt the big cat down before it kills more birds. Everything else continues peacefully. The nights are still cool, although the days now give promise of the hot season that is on the way.

March 23, 1958

Another month has gone by and it seems as if it has been a year. We left for Bangkok to accompany Bob to the airport for his return to the U.S.

When we arrived in Chiengdao on our return we were told that the King's visit had been postponed and that he would come the following day. We were able to hurry around and buy some flags and streamers to decorate our entrance on the road in the King's honor. On Sunday we went to accept the Nai Amphur's invitation to see the King with the local officials when he visited the cave that afternoon. The cave, like the hill tribespeople and the teak lumbering industry, is a leading attraction of the Chiengdao district. It is a long cave in the Chiengdao mountain with beautiful limestone formations of both stalactites and stalagmites. I have spent many hours there exploring the back passageways with flashlight and lantern. It had not as yet been commercialized with an electric generator and ticket fees, guides and souvenirs.

It was a long hot afternoon but I thoroughly enjoyed seeing the royal couple. Everything had been attractively arranged and many people were able to talk to the King and Queen and give them presents. After the royal procession had left we used our jeep to carry the King's gifts to the Nai Amphur's office. On Monday evening the Nai Amphur gave a feast for all his assistants who had helped him with the King's visit. We managed to get ourselves included as well.

April 9, 1958

The hot weather is here in earnest and although the nights remain surprisingly comfortable I do not think there is much doubt that we are in for a very hot season. Nothing particularly exciting has happened these past several weeks and most of the days have been routine. We are still working on the road and preparing the land for oranges and coffee. One evening I had the Nai Amphur and a group of his assistants here for an American-style meal. They are always so nice to me I like to invite them out once in a while. We had chicken, mashed potatoes, and gravy, cherry Jell-O and lemon meringue pie. I do not know if everything was perfectly prepared or if they fell in love with my American cooking, but I do believe they enjoyed having a different kind of meal. Most of them had never had American-style cooking before.

Last Sunday was Easter Sunday and as if to celebrate it Surin, who is now doing all the doctoring in the village, delivered the first of the long expected babies. It was about the easiest birth I have ever heard of. About seven-thirty in the morning Dao reported that Leah was having labor pains but that they were not yet crucial. About nine o'clock just as Twee was beginning his sermon Dao called Surin out of church. As Twee was closing his sermon Surin came back to church. The baby had been delivered during the sermon and everything was fine. It was a little girl and Dao and Leah are very happy; their first child was a boy.

I picked up a couple more little gibbons which the patients caught while out hunting so now I have four. In order to take better care of this expanding family we have built a large wire cage. The cage does not cause any chafing or cuts such as the individual chains sometimes do and it is large enough to give the animals reasonable freedom. Surin and I are continuing with the work on our private orange orchard. Three days a week we hire a small crew to clean the land. We pay them about fifteen cents each a day. This seems inordinately cheap and it is, of course, but wages are extremely low here for unskilled labor. This new land of ours appeals to me more all the time. It is bounded on two sides by water, being situated where a large stream flows into the river. I am already thinking of building myself a house there someday. There is a large, deep pond where the stream connects with the river that will make an ideal swimming pool. Perhaps one day we shall have a paradise here.

The other day Surin and I followed the river down to our new land to learn exactly how it flowed. The trip was fun and gave us an unexpected thrill. As we were splashing along in waist-deep water we heard a crashing sound in the brush to one side of us. Suddenly a king cobra came charging over the riverbank like a mad bull. Apparently it had heard us and taken us for a bird or animal that would make a good meal. When the snake realized its mistake it tried to stop in mid-air, but its momentum carried it right down the embankment and into the river with a splash. Surin and I tried frantically to back away but the current was so strong we could only inch our way in retreat. There were a few tense moments while the twelve-foot length of the snake disappeared under the surface. We held our breath to see which way it would move next. To our extreme relief the dark brown form moved away from us.

Today we are putting a new floor in my house. The old floor keeps drying out and the cracks get so big that anything dropped on the floor vanishes from sight. During the past weeks I have had no mail and it appears as if I have been forgotten at home. But the reason lies probably with the usual after-holiday lull.

May 19, 1958

I have waited so long to write this account that it is difficult to remember all that has happened. The trip south went as planned except for the departure. Gahtoon's wife was supposed to give birth to her child before we left, but nothing had happened yet by the morning of our scheduled departure. Finally, when we had the car all packed and everything ready to go, her labor pains began. We were grumbling and groaning about what to do when suddenly the child was born. Surin tied the cord and cleaned the eyes and mouth and we started on our way as if nothing had happened.

The water-throwing festival of the Thai New Year was in progress so we drove the first hundred miles with our windows closed in order to keep dry. The custom of throwing water on your friends to wish them a happy new year can be pleasant sometimes, but when whole buckets of water are thrown at you inside the car you wonder about the sincerity of the friendship!

We stopped for the night in Nakornsawan as usual and arrived in Bangkok the following afternoon. The next morning, Friday, we went to the agricultural station and paid for the two thousand orange seedlings. In the afternoon we drove to Chonburi again and Surin and I went to the beach. On Friday morning and Saturday we visited a few patients and then went to a clinic where we

126

held a meeting for about a dozen patients. Sunday afternoon we left Chonburi for the north and arrived back at Trinity Village on the evening of Tuesday, April 22.

A few weeks ago there was a big temple fair at the Chiengdao cave temple and I took quite a few movies. The Nai Amphur was pleased to have me take the pictures and I shall try to show them to him some time. I had never really visited a temple fair before and so I was quite interested. There were parades of visitors from nearby temples every day, consisting of priests and dancing girls and papier-mâché floats. They were colorful and made good pictures. One temple parade consisted of a large number of men dressed, painted, and masked to look like the monkey men of Hindu legends. These Hindu legends have been so mixed up with the Buddhist stories that everything is confused now. I had never seen this monkey-man dance before and found it highly entertaining, but I failed to see much religious spirit or significance in the festivities.

Last week we met the Director General of the Public Health Department and the head of the Leprosy Control Division while they were at the Nai Amphur's office in Chiengdao seeking help for their broken-down car. The senior official gave us a lecture about how dangerous and illegal it is for us to issue DDS without supervision of a first-class doctor. Once he had given his lecture he became friendly, and we asked him to visit our village. We have of course followed his advice and we have requested that the government doctors supervise the giving of medication to our patients. I do not expect any change in our procedures, however, because the health officials in Chiengmai are unable to supply a first-class doctor. They have little money and no men.

Life in the colony goes on as usual. Most of our effort has been spent on getting the land ready for the coffee, pineapples, and oranges. We expect the coffee plants to arrive in another week and are already setting in our own pineapple shoots.

June 26, 1958

We have now received our coffee plants and set them in the ground. We received only a thousand seedlings instead of the anticipated two thousand, so both coffee fields are smaller than anticipated. I am afraid that between 10 and 20 per cent of the plants are dying because of careless handling and I feel bad about this. Also we do not really know whether our fields are sufficiently shaded. They may be too shaded. It is difficult when we have to learn by trial and error and I would be grateful to receive some agricultural advice. We have also set in fifteen hundred pineapple shoots and are preparing land to set in a few thousand more. Our problem is that we don't have enough money to buy all we want as quickly as we want. Contributions from outside have fallen off recently. The churches still give regularly but we need most of that money to meet routine expenses in Chonburi. In another two or three weeks we should receive the two thousand orange seedlings from Bangkok. We are trying hard to get the land ready for them but everything grows so fast now during the rains that it is a job to get the fields properly cleared.

Last week when the men were working to clear the land one of them stepped on a python which was curled up and sleeping peacefully. I think it was the same python which has been living here since we moved in. The snake woke up with a start and things were exciting for a while. The men wanted to catch it alive but couldn't figure out how on the spur of the moment. As the snake showed no inclination to give them time, they killed it with hoes and sticks. Surin and I arrived in from a trip to town a few minutes after the massacre and found the monster stretched out in front of Surin's house. As pythons go, it was not a very big one and measured only a little over twelve feet. It weighed probably a hundred pounds. The skin was too badly damaged to make a worthwhile trophy. [It was the first of three pythons we caught in our village.]

I now average three or four scorpion kills a week. Every night before I go to bed it is my habit to have a scorpion hunt. The routine before bedtime goes like this: (1) kill scorpions, (2) undress, (3) clean teeth and wash, (4) have a quick look around for the scorpion I may have missed, (5) get into bed and hope that the first activity has been wholly successful.

Except for the wildlife visitations, nothing unusual has happened in or near our village. The buses and lumber trucks on the road have been involved in a number of accidents recently. We were just behind a lumber truck one day when it turned over and killed a man. Most of the accidents have not involved us much, however; we only see the wreckage a day or so afterward. I am thankful we have our own jeep and do not need to ride the buses and trucks any more.

July 25, 1958

It seems as if we are in the same place as we were last month. Our big project is still waiting to get off the ground because the orange seedlings have not arrived yet. We received a telegram from Bangkok this week saying that they would come during the early part of August instead of in July. Apparently the weather in the Bangkok area has been too dry to take cuttings so there is nothing to do but to wait for more rain. All the land is prepared here and the holes are dug. All we have to do is to put the plants in the ground when they arrive.

Our coffee seedlings seem to be making better progress, thank goodness. When first they were set in they began to wilt and lose leaves and we were afraid many were dead. Recently they have started to bud and push out new leaves and it looks as if most will survive. We have hopes yet that coffee will eventually become a main crop.

As the rainy season progresses and the jungle gets more and more crowded with the maze of underbrush we become more aware of the wildlife again. During the hot dry season most of the wildlife moves away from civilization, only to return with the rains and the protective vegetation. We rarely see more than tracks. A couple of nights ago we lost another chicken to our visiting leopard. I have lost about forty birds to leopards now. Recently we rebuilt the chicken pen, enclosing it completely with walls and a roof; two men actually had their living quarters inside the chicken pen. The big cat decided not to jump over the fence this time. It simply walked up to the wall and pushed some of the bamboo fencing apart. Our two men watched in silent fear and did nothing. The leopard reached in a paw, took out a chicken, and left. The ground was soft and had recently been cleared for a new pineapple field so the next morning we were able to see the leopard's tracks easily. There were in fact tracks of two cats, one of which must have been a cub. The larger tracks were a little over four inches wide.

I have been hearing many stories about the ferocious bears which live in caves in the next mountain range, five hours' walking distance behind our village. Someday we shall have to arrange an expedition to hunt some of these bears. I shall have to try to borrow a .30-caliber rifle because I do not like the idea of hunting bear or leopard with only a .22 to say nothing of our homemade specials. The latter don't always go off, and sometimes they go off in the wrong direction.

A few nights ago I was coming up the hill from Surin's house, strolling along thinking of nothing in particular, when suddenly I became aware of a snake coming down the path. It was only about five feet long but had its head about a foot in the air and looked enormous in the light of my flashlight. Fortunately the snake could not see me behind the glare of the light and merely slowed down and looked around from side to side. It continued leisurely on its way and I gladly disappeared into the undergrowth to let it pass.

August 23, 1958

At last the orange seedlings have arrived and are in the ground but I think we shall lose about 10 per cent of them. The first thousand were dried out by the time we got them and many have died. The second thousand have all survived, however, and it is a wonderful feeling to have them in the ground. For some strange reason it has not rained for more than a week even though this is the middle of the rainy season. The sun has been very hot and the soil is becoming hard and dry. If it does not rain soon our young trees may be in trouble. Many rice farmers, especially in the center of Thailand, have not had enough water to plant their rice. I hope there will not be a crop failure.

A few nights ago one of the bears of which I have been hearing so much strolled into one of our cornfields and helped himself to a few ears. He has not returned but has made everyone nervous. Bears are the only animals that frighten these people. It has always seemed strange to me how they will tackle a tiger, a leopard, or a king cobra without concern or hesitation. But a bear sets them shaking. Of course bears will never run from a man and will often stalk hunters and maul them badly. They appear to be about the size of a large toy panda and no more fearsome-looking except for their terribly long claws.

I spent most of last week flat on my back. Surin says I had pneumonia and has given penicillin for it. I recovered soon so perhaps his treatment was not too far wrong. It is hard to believe that anyone can catch pneumonia in a climate as hot as this but I guess it is fairly common. I really do appreciate Surin. When I am sick he becomes unbelievably good. I could not possibly find a better friend anywhere in the world. If he should leave here I am afraid I would feel completely lost.

We have been out to the government agricultural station at Mae Jo again and collected the rest of our pomelo plants and some lychee seedlings. They are always very pleasant to us at this station and I like to go there. They have given us some cutting from a passion-fruit vine from Hawaii and some other seedlings. I think we now have about thirty different varieties of fruit growing in our village. Time will tell how well they do.

Our jeep does not start so easily as it should. We regularly have the garage in Chiengmai check things but in a few days or so the trouble recurs. I am sure there is only something minor but I wish there were a really excellent mechanic somewhere who could maintain the vehicle properly. Fortunately we have plenty of manpower here so whenever the jeep will not start we simply call out for a dozen or so men and push it until it does go.

For the past few months I have been corresponding with Dr. Wong, my Chinese friend from wartime days. Now he tells me that he thinks he can join me here for a while. This is marvelous news. Not only shall we have a qualified doctor to help us but I shall have another friend to talk to. [Dr. Wong had gone to America for postgraduate medical studies in 1954 and was now a very highly trained physician and surgeon. My father had been his legal sponsor and Dr. Wong had spent his vacations with my parents. He was almost like a brother to me.] Surin is a fine companion, of course, but how nice it will be to have another also. I know it is selfish to think in terms of friends for myself but loneliness is really one of my main problems. I am an American with a good American college education and although I like my leper villagers they can never be intellectual companions for me. Even the local government officials cannot give me the kind of friendship I need. I think the people in the nearby villages look on me as some kind of oddball. I have been offered many girls by the village people who seem to think that I am lonely. But morality apart, I know that such liaisons would never work out. I have to smile and thank them for their concern and express my deep regret that for family reasons I cannot accept. It is all very difficult. One day, I suppose, I shall meet a girl I want to marry but this would create even more problems. How can I ask any woman to share the life of snakes, scorpions, and leprosy? Although there is little danger of my contracting the disease the idea of marrying a man who has lived with lepers for as long as I have is hardly likely to attract many women. Any girl who agrees to marry me would be a wonderful woman indeed. But I must stop thinking about this. As Peanuts said in the comic strip, "There is no problem so great or difficult that it cannot be run away from."

September 28, 1958

It seems that the past month has been spent largely in making and breaking plans to go to Bangkok to meet Wong. He does not seem to be able to get his Thai visa from the Embassy in Washington and we cannot find the source of the trouble. In June we took care of all the arrangements from this end and signed papers of responsibility. We were informed that the visa had definitely been authorized by the main office in Bangkok, and yet the Washington Embassy claims to have heard nothing from them. I do not know where the mix-up has occurred but since my father has been having such a bad time with his heart it is probably a blessing that Wong has been able to stay and doctor him longer.

It is now obvious that our loss in orange seedlings is nearer 25 per cent than the 10 per cent I predicted a month ago. It is good to see the hardy ones growing. We cannot complain too much. We started these orchards on previously unclaimed jungle land and none of us had had any fruit-growing experience. The loss of coffee seedlings has been very slight, but they are unexpectedly slow growing. I am not expert enough at farming to know if this is normal or if they grow slowly because there is too much shade or rain, or too little, or what have you. We shall learn—if we live long enough. Looking at our place as a whole, I think everything looks pretty good now. I know of few places in Thailand that look much better considering the amount of time spent on them.

We put a new set of spark plugs in the jeep and the engine problem seems to be checked for the present. A couple of weeks ago in Chiengmai one of the city buses shot out of a side street and smacked into our left side. Luckily the bus missed the cab and hit only the box and rear fender, which are pretty hard to damage. We reported the accident and spent some time at the police station. The bus driver was fined one hundred *baht* for reckless driving and made responsible for our damage. We did not collect because the bus company holds its drivers responsible for any damages incurred. When we met the poor little driver with his worn shoes and his worried look it was too hard to ask him to pay anything.

October 17, 1958

Dr. Wong finally got all his visas and his papers straight and sailed from San Francisco on September 27. We shall leave on Monday for Bangkok to meet him. It has been at least six months since we were last in Bangkok and it will be a change to go there again. Ahnon and Simoi write that their work in Chonburi seems to be going along normally with no major problems and with a continued increase in patients. Both Ahnon and Simoi seem to be troubled with some personal problems, and so I shall be glad to talk things over with them. I have no idea what their troubles are.

Two of our men were released from jail after serving terms for killing a buffalo. One fellow had to serve one week longer than the other even though they were both arrested at the same time on the same charge. The only explanation given to us is that the clerk wrote down the wrong date for one of them! Since their arrest we have learned of a gang of buffalo rustlers operating in the jungle near us. The buffaloes are privately owned but feed in the jungle. The rustlers catch them and bring them to a point in the jungle near our village and slaughter them there. When people find the bones and remains it looks as if our people have committed the crime. Last night two of our fellows found a fresh kill and we went to the area headman with the report. I do not know if we can expect much action as I think they like to feel our people are guilty of every crime committed in this area.

We have received several warnings about bandit activity. A new bandit gang reportedly has been organized in the neighboring village of Muang Ih. It is said that the price of rice has forced innocent people to become thieves. I am not impressed with this excuse, but the bandits certainly exist. They have robbed a few ox-carts of rice and a few homes. We have been warned to keep a close watch, me in particular, as I am the only foreigner in the area and sooner or later the bandits may try to rob me. Everyone here thinks that all foreigners are rich. I am curious to know what will happen if the bandits do come. We have some tough fellows in the village as well as our homemade rifles but I hope we do not have to fight a shooting war.

Last Tuesday we had a U.S. Information Service show of movies here. It was a pleasant change for our people. We do not feel quite so isolated when we get an occasional diversion from the outside. My existence continues peaceful and routine. I have a lot of ideas for new projects but I am waiting to see what Dr. Wong's plans are so that we can work out new developments together.

This has been a strange rainy season. Despite the long stretches of dry weather, there has been enough rain to keep the crops growing. Nevertheless I think we shall have to begin irrigating when we come back from Bangkok. We have had trouble recently with the laziness of some of the women workers. I have been forced to quadruple their work projects. It's difficult having to be after people to make them work harder. My own disposition seems to be deteriorating rapidly. It seems as if I am always getting worked up over something. When I get mad I cannot speak Thai fast enough to express myself and so I let go a torrent of English which only Surin understands. Poor innocent Surin takes the brunt of everything. He is such a wonderful fellow.

November 22, 1958

On Sunday, October 19, we left Trinity Village for Bangkok. We spent a day in Chiengmai so that the garage could give the car a thorough check. Then on Monday we drove down to Nakornsawan over roads as bad as they had ever been. We spent the night in our old hotel there and heard just before we were going to bed that the government had been overthrown again and that Thailand was now under marshal law. [General Sarit Thanarat had taken over the government again and replaced his previously appointed prime minister. From now until his death in 1965 General Sarit was to be prime minister himself.]

It seems to me that every time we go to Bangkok the government gets overthrown.

On Tuesday afternoon we arrived in Bangkok after being stopped many times by army road blocks. I do not know who they thought was going to march in and take over the government; they surely looked us over carefully. Our .22 rifle caused a little concern although it is legal. Eventually they let us pass, assuming, I suppose, that we could not do very much damage. On arrival we found that Wong's ship was not due until Friday evening and we had two full days to wait. We went to the American Bible Society and collected some Scriptures. These we later left with our workers in Chonburi to give to the patients. We also met in Bangkok our friend Dr. Butler, who was with the U.S.O.M. Malaria Control Program in Chiengmai. He arranged for us to meet some of the top men in the U.S.O.M. Agricultural Division so that we could ask them for assistance. (U.S.O.M. is the overseas designation for A.I.D.—Agency for International Development.) The men there seemed interested in using our place as an experimental farm for their scientific programs. It seems they have difficulty in having their orders carried out on the Thai farms they use and they felt that my living on the farm would assure compliance. They promised to send some experts to test our soil and lay out fields and provide seed and fertilizer. We would get the crops and they would get the publicity value of the demonstration. When we returned to Chiengdao we received a telegram saying that this plan had been indefinitely postponed. I do not know what the reason could possibly have been—none was given—but I do hope that we shall eventually receive some assistance. We can certainly do with some advice.

On Friday evening we drove down to the pier and waited for Wong's ship to arrive. It was a fine new vessel and glided smoothly into sight about eight o'clock just after a beautiful sunset. The customs officials gave the ship a good going-over and then we went aboard to greet Wong. He had been seasick during the journey and was thoroughly happy to come ashore. The customs officials passed all his belongings duty-free and so we loaded the jeep and drove back to the hotel. During the next few days we spent a lot of time getting Wong's business taken care of. We went to the Ministry of Public Health and explained our work in detail. We were most cordially received. Wong had a letter to take to the Immigration Department in Chiengdao. With this letter Wong easily obtained permission to remain in Thailand for an indefinite period.

We took Wong on a sightseeing tour of Bangkok, picked up some medical supplies, and had the jeep checked by the Willys company. Unfortunately the mechanics found many things wrong and we had to pay more than $200, including $35 for a new tire. On Wednesday we took Wong to see our Chonburi work. We visited the cabin on the beach but had no time to swim or lie around. Wong examined Boonkrong's daughter and found that she had TB. I hope she responds well to treatment as she is a dear little girl. We then went to see as many patients as possible in the city and environs of Chonburi. Our men must be doing a good job down there because we met with friendliness and respect wherever we went. Some patients gave us eggs and canned fruit. On Friday we left Chonburi and drove back to Nakornsawan. The road was slightly better this time because there had been less rain. On Saturday night we stayed in Chiengmai and arrived home in Trinity Village early Sunday afternoon.

Nothing of importance had happened in the village during our absence. I am afraid Wong was not very enthusiastic about the prospects of establishing a medical practice in our primitive quarters. He seems to be rather discouraged and I can hardly blame him. He is getting no salary here and he is dubious about the prospects for a paying practice among the people in the other villages; he knows how reluctant they are to pay cash for medical services. I am amazed that Wong ever agreed to come here in the first place, but I do hope we can get some things working right for him. We have made a clinic by enclosing the garage space which is under Surin's house and divided it off into two rooms. Eventually we hope to fix it up so that it has a laboratory, a diagnosis room, and a clinic combined. A cousin of Surin's wife who is staying with them temporarily has done most of the carpentry work for nothing. He is better than any of our fellows and we have been fortunate to have him, even though he loves a good drink and has to be given a few days off every once in a while to recover from a hangover.

Last Sunday was a delightful day for us. Jim Conklin came to preach and brought a group of Karen Christians with him. These Karen tribesmen are the most natural musicians and singers I have ever met. They sang at the church service and gave us a special two-hour concert afterward. Our village people seemed to be as delighted by this as I. The Karens had an endless repertoire of songs in many languages which they sang from memory and in beautiful harmony. It is so unusual to hear singing like this in Asia. Two of the singers were from Burma, the other six from Thailand. They have promised to come back in a few months and give us another concert.

I was just going to have dinner today when a jeep drove in with a man from U.S.O.M. He told me that some of the agricultural project is now on again but it will probably be a couple of months before things get under way. U.S.O.M. has decided to provide some seeds and fertilizer. I anticipate that we shall get substantial help with our fruit and vegetable crops as well as with the food for livestock. In another way today was a sad one. A day-old infant died, making the second death in our village. I was in Chiengmai getting supplies and did not hear about the death until my return. I feel very bad about not having been here at the time but one must get supplies too. Had we been told that the child was ill we would have stayed in the village. These parents rarely bring their children to us unless they are seriously ill or beyond help. I remember another time a few months back when we returned from Chiengmai to find that a child had been born in our absence. The mother had never even told Surin that she was pregnant. When the village was smaller it was possible for us to keep a check on everything that went on. We have nearly three hundred people here now and it is too much to keep track of everybody.

Our coffee seedlings are finally beginning to grow and the oranges and pomelos seem to be doing well too. We have half our garlic field planted and the other half should be planted soon. Apart from the terribly high price we have to pay for rice, everything is doing well. Rice has doubled in price in a year. This would not matter too much if we had steadier, more substantial financing. The present shortage of money is now getting on my nerves. We need so little and yet we never seem to have enough.

December 27, 1958

With the Christmas rush over, I can find time to write again. We had a pleasant Christmas. On Sunday, December 20, the Presbyterian seminary students came up and put on a Christmas program and a pageant for us. On Christmas Eve we sat around a bonfire and ate sticky rice roasted in bamboo sections. Then on Christmas Day Surin, Wong, and I were invited to have dinner in Chiengmai with the Carlsons. We dropped presents off for members of the Nai Amphur's staff on the way and arrived in town in time to attend the service at the Prince Royal College chapel for the English-speaking community. The Carlsons served turkey and all the trimmings; it was wonderful. I do not get tired of rice every day but it does taste good to have a change once in a while. Yesterday, the day after Christmas, a group of eight people from the Overseas Mission Fellowship drove up to conduct a service for us. There were also about twenty people from the Chiengdao church who had accepted our invitation to join us. After the service we had a colony feast of rice and curry. The patients had made two huge twelve-foot balloons of brightly colored tissue paper. The men built small smoking fires and filled the balloons by holding the openings over a bamboo chimney and then they released them. The balloons rose to a height of about two thousand feet and floated slowly over the jungle. They were great fun to watch. It is strange how small things like this make me happy. Perhaps this is because big things never really happen here and anything unusual is exciting.

I have been worrying about how Wong was going to get along financially. But the problem is solved. Yesterday we received $900 from the First Lutheran Church in Albert Lea and a promise to support Wong with at least $100 a month. This has relieved a great deal of tension between us and brightened his prospects and mine considerably. Wong has not much of a private practice yet; most of the local people continue to go to the second-class doctors in their own villages. They wait until they are nearly dead before seeking medical advice. A few days ago Wong had a frantic call to come and look at a small girl. Unfortunately she died a few hours after Wong arrived. There was nothing he could have done, she was so far gone nothing could save her.

We have been planning to set up a small clinic hospital on the main highway adjoining our road. Everything seems to be working out very much better now. The Nai Amphur has promised us legal title to the land and a lumber mill has promised to help with timber. Jim Conklin has sent a gift of $125 to help establish the clinic. He recently lost his three-year-old daughter when she ate a bottle of malaria medicine. They were living in a rural area then, too far away to get medical help in time. We must now decide whether we want to continue our leprosy clinics or whether we want to concentrate on the hospital and the proposed U.S.O.M. experimental farm. Perhaps we can do both but I am afraid our resources are already spread too thin.

The weather during this cold season has been much colder than other years or at least it seems to have been so in Chiengdao. I have heard that in Bangkok it has been unusually hot. We are using all the blankets we own and I use four or five every night. It is nevertheless nice to have cool weather. We have used the pump twice to water the oranges. The hose reaches to the pomelo groves and from there it is connected with a bamboo pipe that reaches to the orange trees. The whole place seems to be coming along fine even if it is taking a long time.

January 23, 1959

We had to shoot my old gibbon this morning. He has been biting people from time to time for several months now but seemed to be friendly most of the time. This morning he deliberately sneaked in and cut a nasty gash in the leg of one of our women patients who was talking to Wong in the clinic. Women seemed to be his special target. This morning was the last straw; I cannot afford to have a gibbon that is going to bite my people. But it is going to seem quiet around here without his howling.

Wong lent me his entire nine months' $900 salary so that we could buy our year's rice supply in advance. I have been wanting to do this every year but I have never had the necessary amount of money at the end of the harvest season. By buying rice at harvest time instead of every week we can save from $300 to $400 in a year. Surin's mother-in-law has built a rice warehouse, but because she doesn't have enough money for rice she has very kindly allowed us to use it to store ours. I have now ordered a small rice mill for hulling and by next week we hope to have the mill set up and running and the rice safely stored away. If everything works out well this should be a great step forward in our village life.

Twee has returned after graduating from Bible School and Dang has returned after his second year. We plan to have these fellows visit the patients in the neighboring villages to deliver the medicine and do any necessary nursing work.

During the week following Christmas we attended the Leprosy Conference at McKean, where Dr. Robert Cochrane gave another series of lectures and demonstrations. This was the first time that I really enjoyed Dr. Cochrane's talk as previously I had always felt he was a little impractical for our limited resources. But on this occasion the lectures were comprehensive and interesting and I think I learned a great deal.

I also enjoyed meeting the other leprosy workers who attended. The course has helped to enlarge our circle of friends a great deal. We met one young lady doctor who graduated last year from school and is now working in the McCormick Hospital in Chiengmai. She has expressed an interest in leprosy and in working in a rural area. Maybe we could get her to assist our work eventually when we finish our proposed hospital here. This Sunday I shall drive a group of nurses and the doctor to visit our village. They may lose their interest, of course, when they see what we have.

We also met and made friends with a young Thai doctor who studied four years in America, specializing in chest surgery. While he was in America he married a girl from Tennessee and she is now trying to adjust to Thai life. Even as a leading chest surgeon in Thailand his salary from the government hospital is only $75 a month plus housing. He picks up a little more on private fees of course but his wife finds their living conditions rather unsatisfactory. American girls who marry Thai men often find it very difficult to adjust to the change in their standard of living.

Dr. Guyer of the McCormick Hospital in Chiengmai has invited Wong to work there for a while so that he can become better acquainted with Thai medical problems and sharpen up his medical practice before taking the government examination for a license. We are now discussing the pros and cons of such a move. As Wong does not have many outside patients here yet and it will be some time before we can establish his new clinic he can undoubtedly do something useful in McCormick Hospital during the waiting period. On the other hand it would be awfully nice to have him here to take care of our own medical problems.

The village remains the same. We water the orange seedlings every week and they are looking very good. The garlic fields are also doing well. Today we are busy building a bridge over the small stream that joins the river in our village. When this bridge is completed we shall have finished a road system which encircles our area. Our main concern is the long wait for the U.S.O.M. people to come and set up their project. I hope they come soon.

February 26, 1959

Wong left here last Tuesday to start work at the McCormick Hospital so I am again alone, at least temporarily. Wong will probably work there for two or three months. I think he will enjoy the opportunity of meeting the nurses and doctors in Chiengmai. We have become quite familiar and friendly with the McCormick Hospital people during these past few weeks and we should get to know even more of them now that Wong has started work there. It is good to make new friends. Dr. Arunee, the lady doctor who showed so much interest in our project, has been exceptionally friendly to us and has agreed to come and work with us as soon as our hospital is ready. This weekend she will come and visit for the third time.

We have been running the rice mill for a couple of weeks but Surin and I feel that we ought to buy a diesel engine before we ruin this little gas engine. Milling is heavy work and there is a lot of dust. The gas engine is air-cooled and it is difficult to find a way of keeping the dust out of the engine. It has also been a nuisance having to change the flywheel every time we change the function of the engine from milling rice to pumping water. We now are going to buy a diesel engine for the rice mill and use the gas engine full time on irrigation. The only problem is finding the money to pay for the diesel engine. We have decided to buy it on credit and I am planning to pay $100 a month. The total cost is $400.

We have quietly been surveying the district to determine how much leprosy is in the area. We have found quite a few cases and some have decided to begin taking medicine. Some, however, are afraid of being discovered by their neighbors. It sometimes calls for a good deal of tact and persuasion to be able to help.

A few weeks ago we discovered an old man who had been so crippled through leprosy he was no longer able to walk. He was living in a small bamboo shelter at the edge of his brother's farm and his brother sent him a bit of food each day to keep him alive.

When leprosy ulcers had become infected years before, he had lost most of both feet. When he could no longer stand upright he had moved about in a sitting position using his hands for locomotion. Over a period of time his hands also had been damaged so that he now had no more than wrist stumps.

We returned to our village and worked with a couple of our wood carvers to devise a special set of crutches for the old fellow. In a few days we returned with the completed crutches. We met him on the path where he was pushing himself along with his hand stumps. We lifted him up and propped a crutch under each arm and used some rubber straps to secure his hands in place on the crutches. At first he could not manage them, but with each step he became a little more confident and finally he was able to set off on his own. He hopped quickly back to his hut and sat there grinning from ear to ear as the sweat poured off him from his exertion. When we visited him again last week he no longer needed a rubber strap for his hands as he had developed a way of propping his arms through the crutches and holding them that way. Now he takes walks into the village to visit his friends.

We also did our first surgery in the village before Wong left for Chiengmai. One of our women patients was due to have a baby but after three days of labor the child just would not appear. The woman was in her thirties and this was her first child and so there was some difficulty. Wong finally decided that the only chance the infant had of being born alive was by Caesarean section. We used a rice steamer to sterilize the instruments and towels, but we did not have enough of any one thing to do the job properly. Wong did the surgery and Surin assisted. I was pressed into service as an anesthetist and a couple of women were made to stand by in readiness to care for the baby. The surgery began simply enough and the patient was drowsy from the effects of morphine and Novocain. Then just as the baby was about to be born we switched her over to ether. Wong had difficulty in getting the child's head out as it was solidly fixed in the pelvis and it was a very close thing for a few minutes whether the child would suffocate, for the placenta was open and no longer performing and the head was stuck and the child could not breathe on its own. The sun had set by now and we had had to call in several volunteers to hold flashlights and lanterns so that Dr. Wong could see to work. Several volunteers gave out at the sight of blood and we had to call in replacements.

Finally the head slipped out and the child gave a choked scream and began breathing. Just two minutes later the patient became temporarily excited before sinking into a deep slumber and her arm slipped suddenly out of the restraint and flopped into the open incision. The sterile field was broken now but Wong remained wonderfully calm as I frantically retied her arm and poured on more ether to get her under again. She then began to gurgle as if she would vomit and I became terribly worried; but she soon quieted and went off to sleep. I am afraid I was a nervous wreck at the end of this performance. It took probably two hours in all. The woman and the little boy are both well and happy, so the operation was a success. No doubt people will say that we have no right to attempt such medical work without the proper equipment and under such appalling conditions. But what should we have done? Let the woman and her baby die?

We still have not heard any more about the U.S.O.M. project. I talked to Mr. William Hussy, the U.S. Consul in Chiengmai, and he promised to check with U.S.O.M. to see whether they are in fact doing anything. He seemed fairly confident that U.S.O.M. would come eventually. Frankly I am beginning to lose interest. The bureaucratic wheels have been turning so long and we have had so many promises that I do not know whether we are coming or going. If people want to help they should help, not make promises they have no intention of keeping.

We water our oranges and pomelos once a week and water the pineapples every other day so the pump is really working overtime. We have constructed bamboo water wheels to irrigate the river-bank gardens of vegetables and garlic. We can't raise the water high enough to reach the citrus orchards, however, and so we are immensely thankful for the pump. In a month we hope to harvest our garlic and onions. The orange trees that Surin planted while I was in America have all blossomed and will bear fruit this year. I am sure the oranges will not be very good, though, as it will be their first year, but it will be wonderful to have any fruit at all.

We borrowed an elephant to drag in the logs for our bridge across the stream and they have been in place for nearly a month now. We still have not completed the bridge supports and the planking. Our men had thirty planks sawed and ready but then they all were burned up in a jungle fire one night. It is now the time when anybody strong enough to light a match feels that he must set fire to the jungle. I am convinced that half the people in this area are pyromaniacs.

March 23, 1959

We began our garlic harvest today and it appears to be a fine crop. The garlic is quite a good size and very few of the plants have died. Surin estimates that we should get about three thousand kilograms (that is, over three tons). We had originally set in two hundred kilograms of small garlic. The harvesting of our garlic means a well-deserved rest for our pump. We are getting so many pineapples that they are taking a lot of water. We should have about five thousand this year. At the moment we have a few pineapples big enough to eat but most of them are only the size of a fist. During the next two months we should be loaded with them. Last week we completed our bridge at last and now have a circular road all the way around the village a mile and a half long. If we add another mile or so for our road to the highway we now have about two and a half miles of roads to maintain with ten bridges. We fixed up a heavy log that can be pulled by two oxen and used as a road grader. It is rather a makeshift arrangement but it seems to be reasonably effective. We have also cut an oxcart road to extend from our village to Surin's and my orchard at Mae Bahm. This is about two miles long and crosses a mountain ridge. I do not think it will ever be usable for a car even if we try to fix it up, but it enables us to send the pump and hose down by oxcart to pump water to the orchards. The river level has dropped so low this year that both our water wheels are now above water and useless.

There are a certain number of legal problems concerned with Dr. Wong's clinic which we had hoped the Nai Amphur would help us solve. Unfortunately he does not seem to have made much progress. Bureaucracy is really a terrible disease in Thailand. I got so fed up that I went to see the provincial governor and told him what our problems were. A few days ago he stopped to visit us. He was very kind and told us to go right ahead with our plans. He said that the necessary forms and permission would undoubtedly follow later and that we need not worry about it too much. During the last two or three weeks we have been felling trees and digging out stumps to prepare the building site for the hospital. There are only four more trees to come down and they will be cut today. Next Wednesday we hope to dig the holes for the foundation posts which we can put in as soon as the lumber company delivers them. We seem to be getting well under way with our plans even though we often hear the people in the Nai Amphur's office and forestry departments complaining that we have not got the necessary pieces of paper to do these things. If we wait for the bureaucratic machine we may die before we achieve anything at all. Fortunately we have found that there will be no water problem at the clinic site. We have dug a well about sixty feet behind the site of the proposed building where the land slopes down to a small rainy-season stream. We found water only three feet down. The well is now eight feet deep and has to be bailed out before the men can dig any more. It is still possible to throw out the water faster than it runs in, however, so we are going to dig deeper. Wong is working in the McCormick Hospital in Chiengmai nearly full time now and comes here only when he has a day off. He is his cheerful self again. I understand he is popular with the nurses and attendants at McCormick, although he cannot speak Thai. He is very modest and pleasant in his manner toward them.

April 23, 1959

Last week our nearest foreign neighbor was shot and killed in Muang Prao. She was Lillian Haymer, an OMF missionary working with the Lisu tribe on the next mountain range east of us. In terms of miles she was quite near but to get to her place we would have to get around the range and it is a journey of several hours. Apparently last week she started down the mountain from her house in the Lisu village to return to her house in Muang Prao. She was accompanied by five carriers. The party had split up during the walk and at one time she was alone. She was shot in the stomach with a shotgun and her body was left slumped on the trail for the two carriers to find when they came up later. Nobody seems to know what the motive was or who was behind it but undoubtedly the police will learn something soon, because they are working hard on the case. There is a rumor that she made herself unpopular by trying to prevent opium growing and smoking. Whether this is true I do not know.

The greatest protection I have in this village is the reputation for toughness that some of our fellows have. A number of the men in the village, although very pleasant to me, are extremely hard on people outside who say anything about their leprosy. Last week was the Thai New Year celebration during which everyone throws water on everyone else. It was also the time for a local custom which allows the men of the area to fight anybody without fear of disciplining from the police. Some of our men went to the neighboring village to buy some extra rice. There they were attacked by a mob who felt it was a good time to teach our people a lesson and put them in their proper leprous place. However, when the dust had settled and the blood had stopped flowing it turned out that our men had half killed the attacking mob. Our man Bahn had pulled up a fence post and used it to flatten about a dozen of the village men. Seeh took a beating but ended up by knifing his chief tormentor and frightening off the others. The headman was about to call for the police—custom or no custom—when he realized that his own people had started the trouble and that our villagers had been defending themselves. Believing perhaps that rough justice was the answer to the problem he let the fight continue. We command even more respect in the area now and this should discourage bandits for another year. In many ways my life here reminds me of stories and films of the American West. There are the good men and the bad men, the rustlers, the bandits, the settlers hacking new lives for themselves out of the jungle, and all the crises of a frontier town. I am not sure where I fit in to all this because I am neither lawman nor gunslinger.

We have started to build our hospital and are working as fast as we can, although by American standards this is not very fast. We got a load of six-by-six beams from the sawmill and set them in as foundation posts about every six feet. Across the tops we have laid beams. The foundations have been painted with oil to preserve the wood. Then six-by-two planks have been put on edge across the supporting beams to form the floor supports. At the moment we have about half of these six-by-two beams in place and have three of the four corner posts set up. Next week we hope to begin setting up two-by-three risers for the walls and then the building should begin to look like a building. We also have bricks for the well and hope to brick up the sides next week. Now that the area has been cleared of brush and stumps it looks very neat. I think we are going to have an attractive clinic.

I heard today that Wong is going to marry Arunee, the Thai doctor. They have worked together so much and have come to like each other so much that marriage seems to be the natural development. It should be a fine arrangement for both of them as they are fine people and will make a good team. Of course, looking at it from the selfish point of view I am hoping that their marriage will be of assistance to the village. A few weeks ago Arunee's mother was operated on at the McCormick Hospital for thyroid trouble. After the operation the family was supposed to replace the blood used during the operation, but they were afraid to donate their blood. They have a large family with healthy children in their twenties; but all were afraid that if they gave their blood they might die. This seems to be a common attitude among the Thai and for this reason it is not always easy to find blood for transfusions. On this occasion I gave some of my own blood for them. I wonder if they object to having mixed blood.

Last week I got so angry with two of our patients that I ordered them to leave the village. Now that I have had time to think the whole thing over I shall probably suggest that they return. Kicking people out does not really solve anything. It merely changes the problem. The point at issue was that the two had deliberately broken a promise they had made to me. The woman is not much good and was married here about a year ago to a tramp of a fellow. They were always fighting and causing trouble. Finally the husband quit the village, leaving his wife pregnant. After Wong had delivered the child the woman said she wanted to marry one of the other fellows in the village. This seemed a good idea and I agreed but said they should wait three months after which we would consider the first marriage dissolved and then she could remarry. The couple agreed to the plan and then, unknown to me, three days later moved in together. I did not find out for some time but when I did I got steaming mad.

I find this whole question of local marriage customs rather worrisome. Perhaps "nonmarriage custom" would be a better expression. Although many the couples live together for years they are often not legally married. It is just too much trouble for many to register. A marriage is not legal unless the couple register at the county seat. Other couples break up and move on to new partners as the mood takes them. Even couples who marry legally can get a divorce simply by applying for it. I know that I have no right to impose my own moral code on these people but this is supposed to be a Christian village and is largely supported by donations from church groups. I think I therefore have a duty to try to regularize their lives somewhat according to Christian standards. At the same time my real purpose is to help leprosy patients lead a normal life. I shall fail in this if I refuse to help people in the village who do not conform to my own moral code. To such problems there are really no solutions. Only compromises.

At last we had a visit from U.S.O.M. Two men came up and looked the place over and promised to send up fertilizers, spray, and seeds. We are now waiting to see what, if anything, will arrive. The village crops look good. The past month has been terribly hot and dry but now we are getting a few showers from time to time. And although it is rather dry, there is enough moisture for us not to have to pump water for our oranges. The pineapples are loaded with fruit but it is still only half developed. Most of our time and energy is spent on the clinic, and according to letters from home this new project is being enthusiastically supported there.

May 21, 1959

The clinic building is finally beginning to look like a hospital and we have received enough money to pay for it. One of the most important developments recently has been the news that the Reverend Knutson at home has definitely decided to help us and is working with a committee of Bob Langemo, Bob Bonnerup, Elmer Falksen, and Bill Kruger to raise money for our hospital. Editor Ken Allen of the Albert Lea *Evening Tribune* has also helped a lot by printing some of my letters about our work. About two weeks ago I received a check for $1000 and another check for $1000 is promised in the near future. This will not provide much equipment but it will certainly ease the situation as far as the building itself is concerned. When I read the way some of my letters have been reprinted in the newspapers at home I am surely glad I am out here and not there. I suppose they have to make a paper hero out of me in order to promote interest in the project, but I wish they would not praise me quite so much.

One of the worst problems in building or doing anything out here is that the men won't follow instructions. They do something wrong. I tell them they have done it wrong and then they waste an hour arguing with me. We are of course both wrong and both right depending on which way you look at it. They are right by their standards and I am right by mine. They want to build a Thai-style building but I do not think a 100% Thai jungle-style building would be suitable for the clinic. We have had good luck as one of the men in Muang Ih has the tools and forms to make cement tiles and he has promised to let us borrow this equipment to make our own roof tiles. This will save us a great deal of money as I am told that two of the men in our village are expert tilemakers. I shall be interested to see if this is true.

Recently a man from a neighboring village was hit on the head by a falling tree in the jungle quite near us and his friends came rushing to us for help. Surin and I went out to see him. The man had chopped down a big tree to catch some kind of animal hidden in the branches. The tree had crashed into a smaller tree on its way down and a part of the smaller tree had splintered off and crushed the man's head. By the time we got to him he had been unconscious for about two hours. He was in very bad shape but still alive, so Surin and I decided to try to get him to Chiengmai hospital where he could receive proper attention. It took two hours for his friends to carry him out of the jungle to our place and put him in the back of the jeep. Then the bumpy ride did not do his broken head any good. We got to Chiengmai about ten-thirty that evening and went to the McCormick Hospital, where Wong was on night call. It was, alas, too late to do anything for him and he died early the next morning. I do not know if it would have made any difference if our own hospital had been ready, although it would certainly have saved him the bumpy jeep ride. Anyway if this is the kind of thing that goes on we shall probably see a lot of such patients when our clinic is eventually opened.

The local people are afraid of the mountain behind us because of the angry spirits they believe are there. These people are obsessed by fear and superstitions. Most of our people are no longer frightened quite so much because they have been exposed to Christian teaching. But even here I hear guns being fired to frighten away spirits whenever a noisy thunderstorm is approaching. There is also an ancient temple ruin in the jungle near Mae Bahm which the area folks are convinced is guarded by a spirit. They will not go near it because they say the spirit is tired of staying there and wants to kill somebody else to take his place. The longer I stay in this area the more I learn about lucky days, unlucky days, magic powders, waters, and spirit offerings. It is interesting but rather pathetic. This fear of spirits fortunately leaves us free to develop a good deal of land areas other people stay clear of.

Wong and Arunee are definitely planning to marry this month. We are beginning to build a house for them near the clinic and Surin's relative has promised to build furniture for them.

June 25, 1959

Wong and Arunee were married on June 2 in Arunee's home town of Payao. Wong had asked a missionary to perform a Christian service but he refused because Arunee is not a Christian, so a Thai civil ceremony was performed which had no connection with either church or temple. I cannot see what good was accomplished by refusing Wong a Christian service but I suppose the missionary is entitled to his opinion. It does seem to me though that too often we are more concerned with the letter of the law rather than with the spirit of love and compassion.

Last week we put the tiles on the hospital roof. They are light green in color but Wong's house will have red tiles. The two patients who have made the tiles have really done a good job. Now we are laying the floor and we shall soon put the walls on and begin the interior finish. It seems the more progress we make with the building the more work needs to be done. It will still be many months before the operating room will be completed. Last Sunday Wong and Arunee and three of their nurse friends came up to look the place over and make suggestions. Their professional standards are higher than mine, of course, and so I was rather discouraged when I heard what they thought of the place. But their advice is extremely valuable and I will do everything possible to incorporate their suggestions into the final building. Wong's house is nearly complete and we shall probably put on the tiles in another week. The furniture which Moo made for Wong is most attractive. He has completed a table and chairs and a bed and a desk and a dressing table for Arunee. Wong seems to be very happy with everything and is great fun to be with. Wong and Arunee are still working in the McCormick Hospital but hope to move up here in July. It will be good to have them here. At the same time I have enjoyed visiting Wong in the McCormick because my visits have given me a chance to become acquainted with many people whom I only knew vaguely before. This has helped much to ease my feelings of loneliness. I have learned a great deal more about Thai customs and Thai interests through my contacts with these friends.

My last little gibbon was killed by one of the colony dogs last week. I had allowed him to run free for several months because he seemed to enjoy it and never bothered anyone. Some of the dogs around here are mean and a group of five of them ambushed the poor little fellow when he was on the ground one day. I was not here at the time, and perhaps it was just as well, because I would surely have shot every dog in the village if I had seen what was going on. I am fed up with them. We now have more dogs than people. The patients say they need watchdogs although there is not anything in their houses worth stealing. I am afraid this incident with the gibbon has not helped my disposition any. Sometimes I get so disgusted with hearing everyone's petty complaints and getting people to do an honest day's work that I feel like leaving the whole bunch of them. If it were not for the joy of working with Surin and Wong and Twee this would be a miserable life indeed.

We are now harvesting several hundred pineapples every week. They are a good size and quite sweet. The market price is not too good at the moment but we should make some profit, which is all to the good since the pineapples have taken very little effort to raise. I also get some bananas every week from my private grove, which I bought from Dao and Leah. And yesterday we noticed fruit on the tung-oil trees for the first time. Our village looks weedy and crude, but we are making progress.

Surin and I have decided to rent a house in Chiengmai where we can stay and save hotel fees on the occasions we have to go in for supplies. We shall pay about $15 a month and have plenty of room and electric light.

July 25, 1959

On July 4, I went on a picnic given by the Americans living in Chiengmai and had a fine time eating baked beans and hot dogs and potato salad. A meal like that tastes awfully good once in a while. On July 5, John White and Khun Arie came up to our village to explain how to use the seeds and fertilizer given us by

156

U.S.O.M. They brought over a ton of chemical fertilizer, sweet-corn seed, and seed for a legume plant to provide nitrogen for the orange field. For the past three weeks we have been busy planting these seeds, putting on fertilizer, and continuing with the construction of Wong's house and the hospital. As we have so many projects our labor force is spread rather thin and nothing is being completed fast. But it is encouraging to have so many new things developing. The U.S.O.M. men and the consular staff are friendly and helpful. Arunee has many friends and some of them come to visit the village from time to time. Most are pleasant, though they seem to feel she is sacrificing too much by living in the jungle. Actually I think her house here will eventually be more comfortable than her friends' homes in Chiengmai.

The other day Dr. Wong and Dr. Arunee had another grue-some case to attend. A woman from a neighboring village was expecting a child and routinely called the village midwife when the labor pains began. When it became apparent that it was not going to be a normal birth and that the infant could not be de-livered, the untrained midwife panicked. Lacking the skill to save the child, she frantically tried to save the mother. In her own crude way she tried to cut out the infant and succeeded in remov-ing half of the poor dead body.

For three days the tortured mother lay with the remains of her infant. When the odor of rot and death had permeated the entire area, she was finally carried to Dr. Wong at our clinic. He and Dr. Arunee removed the remains of the child and cleaned up the woman. Before she left she appeared well enough to look for-ward to bearing more children at some future time.

I used to smile as I listened to the patients describe their afflic-tions. Invariably their histories included comments about "bad wind" in them somewhere. Bad wind seemed to be the root of all their problems. This didn't mean a shortness of breath but simply evil wind.

Getting accurate medical histories was next to impossible

through the doctor interview. Many women swore up and down they were ten or more months pregnant and yet didn't give birth for another month or two. I marveled at Dr. Wong's good-humored patience.

August 18, 1959

It seems as if we are going to be building the clinic for the rest of our lives. When I look back over the entries in this book and read my optimistic statements I wonder what's wrong with me. We make progress, I suppose, but only from one job to another. I now have no idea when the clinic will be finished. On Sunday evening after supper a couple of fellows came tearing in on their bikes and asked us to help a seriously sick man in another village. The man had cut his toe a few weeks earlier and the local public-health doctor had been treating the infection. On Sunday the doctor realized that the man was about to die of tetanus and he sent to us for help. Wong and Arunee had already left for Chiengmai and we had no antitoxin on hand here, so there was nothing we could do but load the patient onto the jeep and drive him to Chiengmai. We learned later that he died there.

September 26, 1959

I have finally had definite word that Paul Larson is coming. [Paul is a young man from Northfield, Minnesota, who once heard me speak and saw my films in his home church. He later met Bob Mortenson after Bob's return to the U.S. Paul had been attending Dana College but wasn't sure of his future goals and so wanted to spend a winter here to help get a better perspective on his life.] He left the U.S. on September 14 on the MS *Castleville* and is expected to arrive in Bangkok about the middle of next month. We have not decided yet whether we shall go to Bangkok to meet him. Of course it would be the proper thing to do but we are so short of money that I hate to spend anything on a trip.

Last Sunday we changed our village work policy. We had planned this change for some time but did not expect to make it for another few weeks. However, last Sunday the people voted to make the change immediately. The new policy is that we shall provide rice for only a few old men and some cripples. The rest of the people will buy their rice with money they earn working for themselves or for me. I take over the orchard and fields and pay wages for the upkeep but can retain all profit for colony use. We now have about twenty men working for wages and the others are working on their own projects. I pay fifteen cents a day. I think the total costs will run about the same, but the quality of the work should improve as the men will have more incentive. The men who can work full time to support themselves will also feel freer and stronger than before. This is a halfway step to that of the village becoming completely self-supporting. We continue to provide medical care free of charge and such common drugs as aspirin, sodamint, and sulfa. Unless the case is extremely serious, the patient will have to pay for special medicines. I have had to make this decision because the patients have demanded expensive drugs for the mildest of ailments.

The clinic is still not completed although two of the rooms are now ready for use. We hope to finish things in a hurry once we have finished worrying about Wong's house. As soon as we put in a few more screens he and Arunee can move in.

October 9, 1959

The past few days have been rather hectic so I'll try to get all the events down before I forget something. On Tuesday Wong and Arunee moved into their new house and we spent most of the day hauling their stuff and getting it arranged. Early on Wednesday morning Surin had a slight heart attack which sent up his blood pressure and caused a slight heart murmur. Wong didn't think it would be serious if Surin would take things easy for a week or so. Since this advice was given Surin has hardly had a spare moment to catch his breath!

On Wednesday afternoon the U.S.O.M. men came to see us again. John White is going home so he brought his replacement to see us. They offered to help develop our irrigation system and improve the vegetable and potato crops. Surin and I were much encouraged by their interest. Our village was not too trim and clean for them but the fellows seemed to feel that with the help we have we do very well. If these U.S.O.M. fellows are typical of men working on the Foreign Aid program, I cannot understand why there is so much criticism of government officials. [I must add here that after John left the country, help from U.S.O.M. gradually dropped off to nothing.]

On Wednesday night, a little before midnight, I woke up to hear somebody shouting Surin's name. I had rolled over and fallen asleep again when Wong came panting up the hill calling my name. He pounded on my door. There was a robber, he screamed, and I thought for a moment somebody was chasing him. When he calmed down I got the story a little clearer. Sang Wong, one of the two watchmen, had awakened him to say he was sorry but he had just killed a prowler who had attacked him. Wong and Arunee heard the word "prowler" and panicked. After one brief look toward the prowler's body which Sang Wong was pointing out, they picked up my .22 rifle, a knife, and a flashlight and ran the mile to our village. Arunee stayed with Surin's family while Wong, Surin, and I drove out to the hospital in the jeep. Wong examined the prowler and found that he was dead from loss of blood from wounds on the face and neck. The wounds had been inflicted with an ax. We listened to the story again and then drove to Chiengdao to inform the police.

Apparently at about seven-thirty in the evening, just as Chan and I were leaving Wong's house, a stranger had strolled in. We had hesitated just long enough to see whether he wanted a ride to the village with us, and then left. But he had come to look the village over, find out where we kept our tools, and size up our two watchmen. A few hours later he returned to attack them while they were sleeping in their small bamboo house. Sang Pong woke up when the intruder came in. He poked Sang Wong to wake him and then hurled his wooden pillow at the prowler. Sang Wong flicked on his flashlight just in time to see the fellow swing a club down through the mosquito net and onto his upper leg. Sang Wong grabbed the small ax which he took to bed with him every night and struck at the intruder, hitting him in the mouth with the blade. Sang Wong and Sang Pong then hurled themselves at the man and slashed and struck him until he dropped. Then they went to call Wong and Arunee.

We spent the rest of the night talking to the police and the area headman. I drove to Chiengdao twice and to Muang Ih twice before daylight and finally got to bed about eight that morning. At ten I was called to take the police and Sang Wong and Sang Pong into the Chiengdao police station. The police seemed to accept that our men had killed the intruder in self-defense.

Today, however, the dead man has been identified as a hoodlum from a village ten or fifteen miles north of us who is wanted as a key witness in a huge teak theft now being investigated. The police are now looking at the murder in a different light. Apparently they had been instructed by the provincial governor to protect this man from any possible harm. Now that he is dead the police are embarrassed because they failed in their duty. I think they are trying to cover themselves by suggesting that the man was murdered rather than killed in self-defense. The police are certainly making difficulties about releasing Sang Wong and Sang Pong and I am very worried that they may be arraigned on murder charges.

November 24, 1959

After the first few days of excitement following the death of the thief, things have settled down. Wong and Arunee were so upset that they have taken a three weeks' vacation in Arunee's home town, and Surin and I went to Bangkok to meet Paul. Surin had never flown before and so we decided to make the most of our opportunities and go to Bangkok by plane. We left Chiengmai by a Thai Airways two-engine plane about two in the afternoon and arrived in Bangkok four hours later after stopping en route at Lampang and Sukhothai. The flight was surprisingly smooth and I think Surin enjoyed himself a great deal. Paul's ship was a little behind schedule and so we spent the time running around trying to clear our new DDS shipment through customs. It was a stroke of luck for us that we had received word of the shipment and its arrival in customs just before leaving for Bangkok. We also heard that we had received unexpected donations which enabled us to make the trip. The customhouse was just the same as before. Everyone was extremely pleasant and helpful and yet it took two days and much mileage before we could get things cleared. Paul's ship arrived at noon on Saturday, November 17. We spent the rest of Saturday and all of Sunday showing him some temples and shops and places of interest and finally left on Monday evening by express train to Chiengmai. While we were in Bangkok Surin and I visited the U.S.O.M. fellows again and got more promises of aid.

We also talked with Ronald Hill, the Southern Baptist missionary now in Chonburi, about the Baptists' taking over the Chonburi leprosy work we started. Hill was very nice and eager to take over our work. The Baptist Board has now officially taken on the work and we have agreed to let Simoi continue working there to help them. And so ends another of our little leprosy projects. We provided care and treatment for well over five hundred patients there for three years. We spent over $2500 on the work there plus the medicines.

Since coming to Chiengdao Paul has proved a fine addition to our team. He is pleasant and uncomplaining and a very willing worker. He should be a wonderful help to us. Wong and Arunee returned the day after Thanksgiving services and settled once more in their house. We have sent out a few more men to sleep there at night and so they seem quite contented.

Last week Wong and Arunee performed a Caesarean delivery on a woman from the neighboring village of Muang Ih; she had been in labor for three days and was nearly dead when brought in. Wong had been a little hesitant to do surgery here but in this case he had no choice. Arunee assisted and Surin gave the anesthetic while Paul and I did what simple tasks might be useful. This was the first surgery performed in the new hospital and so special mention has to be made of it. Though the walls and ceiling were still a bit rough, the patient was able to settle down comfortably in the ward after her surgery. In the first evening she had eighteen visitors crowding in the room to see her. Two days later Wong cut out an old chronic ulcer from one of our patients that had come up from Chonburi. Now we have two patients in our hospital before it is even finished.

Last week was the Festival of Lights—the Loi Kratong—in Chiengmai and we took Paul to see it. The small candlelit floats going down the river by the thousands were a beautiful sight.

Paul and I are now helping to organize a basketball team in Chiengdao. Basketball has become popular in Thailand and every winter there is a big tournament at the Chiengmai Winter Fair. The Chiengdao people are enthusiastic and it should be a good way to make friends with them as well as to get some extra exercise, as if we needed it.

December 19, 1959

As usual during the week before Christmas things are getting busy; I had therefore better write while I have the chance. Actually this will be about the easiest Christmas I have had out here as Twee is taking care of many of the details. He has arranged for most of the meetings and the village banquet and a good part of the village decorations. I have only had to buy colored paper and some cookies and candy. What a joy it is to have fellows like Surin and Twee to work with. We have begun the construction of a small house near the hospital where Boonkrong can live temporarily and which can be used as a nurses' home later on.

The basketball team we formed in Chiengdao seems to be improving all the time. For a while everyone seemed to think that our team didn't have much chance and they hated to embarrass themselves by playing with us. Now they seem to think we have a very good chance and tomorrow afternoon we shall have a practice game with a team in Chiengmai which will give us a better idea of what our future chances will be. If we can only beat a few teams I think this basketball idea may help us to make many new friends in the Chiengdao area. The people are looking for something to boast about and our team may be the very thing for them. We still have ten days before the Winter Fair tournament and our fellows learn quickly. I am sure they will soon be in good form, for Thai people are wonderfully well coordinated.

January 21, 1960

A month has passed since I last wrote and quite a few things have happened. After our Christmas festivities we went to Chiengmai to play basketball with the Chiengdao team in the Winter Fair tournament. In the opening game of the tournament we

164

played the team which was the big favorite to win. With one minute left to play, the score was tied 44–44, before our fellows made three consecutive bad passes and we lost 50–46. We then went on to win the next three games we played and won third place in the final standings. The Chiengdao people were thrilled and we made a lot of new friends all around. We have been invited to take part in a big tournament to be held during the Thai New Year celebration in a couple of months' time.

Last Tuesday we had the court hearing for Sang Wong. [Sang Pong had been cleared earlier.] He has been held in prison without charges for over three months while the CID inspectors have investigated the case. The judge ruled that Sang Wong may have been a bit too severe in defending himself and sentenced him to eight months for manslaughter. But this sentence is automatically cut in half, since Sang Wong confessed to the "crime" in the first place. This means that he has only another few weeks to serve.

We haven't completed the irrigation system for the orange grove yet. All the pipes and connections and faucets are laid, however, and the next job is the cementing. We are now preparing bamboo for the cement forms. When we get the rock and sand ready we can mix cement and get the project done. Nothing is fast or easy for us, of course, so it may be weeks before we are through. I can't think of anything else that is important enough to write about. Life is as peaceful and quiet as always, even though there are always tales going around of opium and teakwood murders and a host of other things. I often wonder how I always manage to miss the excitement in life and only read about it.

March 3, 1960

We finally began pouring cement for the water tank this morning. It has taken a lot of time and work to get all the rock and sand to the top of the hill because the tank is really quite big and uses a lot of cement. We had an unexpected week of heavy rain in the first part of this month and our work has been slowed down but the rain did the orange trees a lot of good. We are just beginning to be able to eat the fruit which is ripe on the first thirty trees planted three and a half years ago. The fruit seems to be quite sweet. If this fruit is typical of the orange crops to come, we should do very well. I never realized before how small orange trees are or how loaded with fruit they get. Every day we have expanded our pineapple field. We have several workers who do nothing but cut off new pineapple shoots and transplant them. Our bananas are sprouting new shoots at a faster rate than we can transplant them. We'll soon have tens of thousands of these. Our clinic project goes slowly, but progress is being made.

Sang Wong was released from prison several weeks ago and seems to be happy and as busy as a bee working all over the place. Dao and Boonkrong are working equally hard. Boonkrong's house is nearly completed. This week we hope to complete the septic tank and toilet and Boonkrong should be able to move in soon. Wong and Arunee took a two-week vacation in Payao but they are back again now and seem to be doing quite a good business.

People tell me that Wong and Arunee are going to leave Chiengdao but I haven't heard anything from Wong that indicates he has any such plans. I don't know whether to mention the rumors to him. There is no doubt that there is a great need for a doctor in this area. Unfortunately I think Wong and Arunee probably find the life hard and unrewarding in many ways. Boonkrong is doing fine and makes up for any discouragement given me by the doctors. He is also so popular with the various mission groups that I don't know whether I shall be able to keep him here. The Alliance want to send him to a Philippine Bible school and then retain him as a teacher at their Thailand schools. The Baptists want him as pastor for their Chonburi church and the Presbyterians also want his services. Boonkrong keeps his own counsel so I never really know what he is thinking. [He shortly afterward accepted the Baptist invitation and moved back to Chonburi to work with them.]

Surin is building a new house on some land he has cleared south of the hospital. I continue to marvel at what a fellow Surin is. He works harder and longer than anybody else and yet he manages to develop these private projects on the side. His wife and mother-in-law and brother all help, of course, but even so his achievements are often unbelievable. Twee is also busy with a multitude of projects. He is building a new house, digging a well, and developing garlic fields and pineapple fields.

April 12, 1960

The hospital is completely finished and painted inside and now we have four beds, mattresses and pillows, etc., for the wards. Moo has been working on furniture this past month and has made most of the chairs, stools, and tables that we shall need. He is now working on an operating table which Wong has designed. Wong and Arunee seem to be happy and when they are in a good mood they are as fine as anyone can possibly be. More and more emergencies are brought into us all the time and Wong does a good job with them. One small child died last week in the hospital and was our first death in the new building. The child had been here only about half an hour before it died so it was almost beyond help.

This week there has been a temple fair at the Chiengdao cave. Wong has been the doctor for the boxing matches. There have been some excellent fights and I enjoyed watching them. It is good for Wong to meet more people and become better known. One night they had international-style boxing and I was asked to be the referee. It was a lot of fun.

Several nights ago as we were coming home from the fair the brake-fluid line developed a leak and our brakes went out. Nothing serious happened luckily but when we arrived at our hospital area two men were waiting for Wong and begged us to drive to Muang Ih right away to see a fellow who had been attacked by a bear.

I forgot all about brake trouble when I saw the poor fellow who had been attacked by the bear. He was lying propped up on pillows. Half of his face had been torn away and part of his brain was exposed. One eyeball was hanging out and his tongue was visible through a gap in his cheek where the cheek bone had been torn out. His chest was ripped open and the air rushed in and out of it as he breathed. He had insufficient blood to register any pulse or blood pressure and so of course he was no longer bleeding from the gaping wounds. Wong could not promise to save him even though the man was still conscious and able to answer questions rationally in a weak voice. Since they felt the man was going to die, his people decided not to let him go to the hospital where Wong could try to patch him up. The local superstition is that if a man dies away from his home his spirit will become confused and angry.

Last month I myself had a little episode in the hospital. I had been bleeding from the rectum and so finally had Wong examine me. He suggested that I should go to the McCormick Hospital in Chiengmai, and I did. At McCormick they checked first of all for the cause and decided it was more from hemorrhoids than from dysentery ulcers. My first surgery almost turned out to be my last. I was given a spinal anesthetic and felt fine for a while. Then suddenly I became sick. I suppose I must have had some kind of reaction to the spinal, because my blood pressure dropped and I went into shock. They had to give me oxygen and stimulants. At the time I felt very dull and hazy as if everything that was happening didn't concern me. After the surgery I spent a week in the hospital and had a wonderful time. The student nurses were as nice as they could be and the food and service were excellent.

Actually I have heard lots of complaints about McCormick but I found everything wonderful. Of course I am not so critical of things as I used to be. I had severe headaches for about two weeks as a result of the spinal but they cleared up and now I am fine.

We seem to break a spring every month now in the jeep and I can't understand why. It is true that the roads are terrible and we do have heavy loads sometimes but I drive very carefully.

We have finished the concrete reservoir and connected all the plastic pipes and are now working on a pump house near the river. Eventually I think we should have a good irrigation system despite our current troubles. The plastic pipe keeps coming apart and draining the tank and we can't get everything tight enough. I think we will have to reconnect all the pipes again. At Mae Bahm we are using brick from an old temple ruin to build the reservoir. There isn't enough brick for the whole thing but there is enough to save us a good deal of cement. If I ever build a house in Mae Bahm I think the old temple site will be ideal. The river makes a loop and could be seen on both sides of my house. I may never build it but I can dream about what a lovely location this would be.

Paul Larson left for America in order to earn some money before returning to college in the fall. We shall miss him.

May 7, 1960

When we arrived back in Trinity Village from a trip we heard that the Muang Ih bear had returned and killed two more hunters, raising his score to three. We also heard that the bear has been chased out of that area and has moved across the road into ours. Our people are now keen on looking for bears and in fact did locate one in a small cave near our village only a couple of days after we returned. They called out a couple of our best hunters who rushed off with their homemade rifles to do battle. Luckily for us the bear was a female with two cubs and she tried to defend the cubs in the cave first before she turned on the hunters. This gave our men the chance to shoot her six times and finally kill her. If she could have rushed from the cave at the first shot she may well have killed one of our men, as a shot or two isn't usually enough to stop a bear. Anyway the men proudly carried her back to the village, skinned her, and sold the meat. One cub was killed in the fight but the other one is healthy and is now my pet. I don't know what I shall do with the bear when it grows up. He may make a good watchdog, but then I suspect I shall need somebody to watch the bear.

I had planned to stay here for another year before returning home but I received a letter from my brother Jim last week asking me to come home this summer as Mother is not well. There have been several vague hints about her health in recent letters from home but until now no one has suggested that her illness is serious enough to demand my coming home. Jim's letter worries me and I have decided to go home as soon as I can get everything organized here. Surin plans to come with me and this means that we have to get everything doubly well taken care of before we leave. We have decided to have Charn take care of the budget and the work projects and to leave Twee in charge of the spiritual work. Wong and Arunee will continue to be in charge of the clinic and medical work. Actually most of our people are already so independent that I rarely see them any more. I don't think they will miss me one little bit although I feel they will miss Surin a lot. The village now has its own governing body and its own church committee, and handles all village and church activities without any help from me. Most of the people are supporting themselves and don't ask for anything except medical help. The few cripples we do have working on the village crop can easily be taken care of by Charn.

May 24, 1960

I am all packed and ready to leave tomorrow. The past two weeks have been a real rush but I am confident that everything will be well taken care of while I am away. My little bear cub accidentally hanged himself on his chain one day while I was in Chiengmai and so we don't have him to plan for.

Surin has all his papers ready and approved for his visa including a statement from Dr. Chinda that he is free of any leprosy. We were not quite sure what to expect from Dr. Chinda, but when he saw all of Surin's smears come up negative Dr. Chinda was as nice as could be and wrote a most useful letter.

Our pineapples are now ripening by the hundreds and are delicious. Our bananas are also fine and the orange trees lush and beautiful. I have at the moment only one piece of unfinished business. This is with Ajana.

Chapter 6

The previous chapters in this book have been an edited version of the three diaries I kept from the time I first came to Thailand to the end of 1962. Although I have cut out quite a lot of material—I tended to be repetitive about my encounters with snakes—I have not put anything in (except a few bracketed notes). It is always easy to be wise after an event, and it seemed better to let our mistakes speak for themselves.

I was rather startled to discover what little mention the diaries made of Ajana, the girl who became my wife and the mother of my two children. During the time covered by the third diary Ajana was the most important thing in my life and my greatest problem. And yet I find that I hardly referred to her. Although I am rather hazy about my thinking at that time, the omission must have been deliberate. Why this was so I do not know. I can only guess that I may have felt that to put down my feelings about Ajana in cold print would be to tempt Providence. Perhaps I did not want to risk being reminded of her if all our plans went wrong. Another reason may be that throughout the diaries I had kept the contents very matter-of-fact and held introspection to a minimum. The diaries give little indication of my state of mind during some of the long and tedious periods of doubt. They do not reflect my own self-doubts, my fears for my future, or my fury at the obstructionism I had to overcome from various quarters. Neither do they reflect the almost total disillusionment I experienced when dealing with organized religious groups. People are fine individually, but put them together on a committee and they become different.

I met Ajana at a time when the project was at an all-time low so far as future developments were concerned. The village itself was a success and had become self-supporting. There was nothing more for me to do except start another village. But there was no organization to help me. Neither Surin, without whom I would be lost, nor I could face the thought of starting another village without proper financing. We had both worked too hard for too long to go through it all again. We had, we felt, proved our point. Trinity showed that we had not been overly optimistic. But it had been a long uphill slog. If we were to do it again we wanted sufficient help to be able to cut the rougher corners.

It was my custom when in Chiengmai to call at the U.S.I.S. library. They had a fair range of magazines and a small but useful library of books I could borrow. One day when I went in, Ajana was there talking to her friend Supank, the librarian. I had seen Ajana once before, waiting outside one of the local theaters with her father Dr. Arie, who was one of the first foreign-trained psychiatrists in Thailand, and now in charge of the mental-health program of the ten northern provinces. Although I had been introduced to Dr. Arie many years back by Dr. Buker, I had never sought him out again. And when I saw him with Ajana that first time, I was so taken by her that I did not dare go up and reintroduce myself. If Ajana hadn't been with him, no doubt I would have gone up and said hello. But the fact that he had this lovely thing with him tied me all up and I walked quietly by.

When I saw her in the library, I had, I guess, been daydreaming a bit about her. I had had no real girl friend all the time I had been in Thailand and my feelings were a bit pent up one way and another. Ajana had looked like just the kind of girl I wanted to meet, and now here she was in the library. I was with Surin and Paul Larson at the time, and as we walked into the library I grinned in Ajana's direction. Her nose went higher in the air than mine ever could have gone, and that was the end of that.

Time went by and I was in the U.S.I.S. library again. Ajana was talking to Supank. I went over, dressed to kill in baggy khaki trousers and a T shirt with the dust of Siam over me, and asked Supank to introduce me. She muttered something and I shot Ajana the usual line about where do you come from and what do you do. After a little conversational fumbling and one or two false starts we found ourselves not just making social chat but actually talking. We moved over to some armchairs and talked nonstop for more than two hours. I don't like to be unkind to Thai women because they are sweet and gentle, but Ajana was the first Thai girl I had met who had anything to say, or perhaps I should say was able to listen intelligently to what I had to say. But that would be unfair to us both. She had been to America to study music and so we had common ground there.

Although it is not too difficult to get talking to a Thai girl of good family and education, it is almost impossible to make further progress. They are protected and chaperoned; they are spied on and their every movement reported back to parental headquarters. It is difficult enough for a Thai man to make progress but for a *farang* (foreigner) it is a labor of Hercules. Even if the Thai man is accepted as a financial and genetic possibility, so to speak, he still has no opportunity to spend any time alone with his girl. The only time they get to meet when the parents are not noting down every syllable is at parties. The "I love you" bits, if they get expressed at all, are slipped in somewhere between the soup and the dessert. The foreigner suffers from the added disadvantage of being highly suspect. The parents worry, naturally enough, that a foreigner might want to marry their daughter. They are even more worried that he might not. Once a Thai girl is seen with a foreigner her reputation is shattered beyond repair. Her value in the marriage market is something that can be offered only in the bargain basement. As is the case everywhere, but more so in Thailand, it's not what you do that matters, it's what people think you are doing. And usually people think you are doing what they would do if they had half the chance.

Had Ajana not been to America and had she not been in a state of active rebellion against her parents and the restrictions of Thai custom, I would never have had a chance. Fortunately, for me, she was not happy at home. Although she loved her parents dearly she wanted to decide her own future. A fiancé had been chosen for her on the basis that he was a pleasant young man from a good family with good prospects. What more, it was argued, could a girl want? Ajana wanted a great deal more, in particular the right to make her own mistakes.

Risking all, I invited her to have lunch with me at one of the local restaurants. She accepted and we went off together to have a plate of sinful unchaperoned noodles. During lunch Ajana explained that she was supposed to be at a dressmaking class. She hated dressmaking but had taken it up as it provided a reason for going out of the house alone. During lunch, which was a nervous occasion as Ajana was sure someone would see us and report back to her father, we talked more. I tried to convince her that although my appearance belied the fact, I had at some time in the past received an education and knew the difference between a spoon and fork. Six years in the jungle had not improved my display of the social graces.

After lunch I took her back to the U.S.I.S. library. We had only just got back when there was a phone call from her mother, who had been phoning around town for hours, saying that Ajana's fiancé had arrived on the morning plane. Ajana was to come home immediately. The car would call for her in ten minutes.

Our next meeting took place a few days later. I went to the little sewing shop where she took lessons. Ajana came out, having made the sewing teacher promise to cover for her, and we went into a nearby café for a Pepsi and a talk. Then Ajana went back to the dressmaker and sewed like mad until her father's car came to pick her up. Our courtship was conducted from about ten-thirty to eleven-thirty three mornings a week. I wanted to call on her at home but she pleaded with me not to. While her parents were not sure what was going on they would do nothing and hope for the best. Once they knew, they would do everything possible to put a stop to our relationship. I have no doubt that they would have succeeded. Her father is and was an important man locally and had he wanted to he could have made life very difficult for me. It is so easy for an error to be suddenly discovered in an alien's documents.

Then, perhaps realizing that if our relationship was to be given a chance to develop, something fairly drastic had to be done, Ajana informed me that she was going to live in Bangkok with her uncle. Her parents tried to dissuade her and there was the usual fight about "Why do you want to leave home?" But Ajana was a determined young lady and as she promised to stay with her uncle her parents did nothing to stop her. When she had been in Bangkok a few weeks she got a job with the Southern Baptist Mission as a translator. She had been converted to Christianity many years before while a pupil at the mission school in Chiengmai. Her religion was another reason for her problems with her parents, both of whom were devout Buddhists.

I wanted badly to go to Bangkok to talk to her but had insufficient money. Paul Larson came to my rescue and made a trip possible.

Thai girls in Bangkok have more freedom than they do in the provinces. We were able to meet for evening meals in restaurants and go to the movies a few times.

No relationship can stand still. Ajana and I both knew this. We had either to think about marriage or to say good-by and forget the whole thing. I had never had any intention of marrying a Thai girl. I knew nothing of the problems of marriage, and certainly nothing of the problems of a mixed marriage, but I had always assumed that to marry a girl of another race would compound the normal problems. But Ajana was, well, Ajana. When you find the girl you want to marry you forget about little racial differences. You don't notice that her background is wholly different from your own. If you do, it just adds to the interest. Ajana was intelligent and had had a good education. I could see no reason why a marriage would not work. Also, unlike so many Thai girls, she was good at socializing. She had the confidence and social ease of any American girl. And yet she had all the charm of Thai women. She was graceful and less pushing than so many American women. She never tried to dominate a conversation. She was also just that much more feminine than any woman I had ever met before. Asian women in general, I think, find their greatest satisfaction in life from loving a man and being loved in return. If a woman's husband shines in his profession she is naturally happy for him. If he does not it is of no importance. It is only when the love has gone out of a marriage that an Asian woman becomes concerned with status and material possessions.

My six years or so in the jungle had made me a realist. I had had more than enough thinking time. One thing that attracted me to the idea of marrying a Thai now that I found myself facing the prospect was that Thai women age so well. Old ladies are as slim and graceful as young girls. I am not talking of the peasants, who age terribly quickly under the hot sun, but of the professional classes. Many Thai women of forty who have had four or five children look about twenty-five.

Marriage customs and sexual morality in Thailand are changing slowly. The man is still king with total freedom. Before marriage he seeks physical relief with paid prostitutes. There are brothels of all kinds in every town and no shame is attached to visiting them. There is no physical contact at all between engaged couples and the girl is well aware that when her young man leaves her after their chaperoned meeting he will probably go straight to the brothel. I have even heard a girl tell her fiancé to have a good time. Sex is a purchasable pleasure. "Having a woman" is comparable to having a meal in a good restaurant or going to the movies. In Thailand women are divided into two kinds: "good" and "bad." Supposedly the good ones you marry; the bad ones you buy sex from.

After marriage the men continue to exercise their freedom of sexual activity. Although foreign-educated and professional Thai women are beginning to make difficulties about this, it is still exceptional for a Thai wife to voice objection to her husband's buying sex. What she feels is another matter. Custom dictates that she should not care. No doubt many women have conditioned themselves into not caring. The many women who do not love their husbands and do not want to be bothered by them are probably grateful for the custom. Women who do love their husbands and who experience happiness in their married lovemaking must care a great deal.

At one time polygamy was legal and usual. Now it is illegal and still usual. Many men, particularly men in business, take "secondary wives." In our terminology these wives would be called mistresses or kept women. In fact they are set up with houses and cars: they produce children who are legally accepted by the father, and they lead perfectly respectable social lives. It is only at official functions that the real wife is in the ascendancy, so to speak. The real wife will usually concern herself with obtaining security for herself and her children when faced with this kind of competition.

Needless to say, the wife has no sexual freedom. In Thailand the double standard operates as effectively as it does in Japan.

Ajana, I think, could not face the disappointments of a normal Thai marriage. She had revolted against her parents and she had revolted against the virtual subjection of Thai women to the demands of their husbands' selfishness. I soon believed that if I asked her to marry me she would say yes. For a few months there was no need for me to rush things. True she was in Bangkok and

I was in Chiengdao, but I was not a love-struck boy. I was thirty and had been living alone for a long time. I was in no hurry.

Then came the news that my mother was more seriously ill than I had at first been led to believe. I knew I had to return to America. I knew, too, that Ajana was unhappy. If I went to America without her it might be years before I could return to Thailand. I had no right to ask her to wait for me indefinitely. Promises are all very well, but Ajana would have to face daily stories from friends and relations of the hundreds of foreigners who had kidded Thai girls along and then left them. Most foreigners who get involved with Thai girls do so with the butterflies of Bangkok —the hostesses in the bars. When the foreigner gets home he realizes that magnificent though his girl friend may have been she would hardly fit in on Main Street U.S.A. The fact that Ajana was different and that our whole relationship was different from the normal Thai-*farang* relationship would do little to ease her fears and doubts when her friends started talking.

I wrote to Ajana, told her about my mother and that I would have to leave soon. I asked her to marry me and come home with me. At first she would not commit herself. It was too soon. Finally she agreed but asked that we go to America separately and be married there. She thought that her parents might be able to stop a Thai marriage but that if she went to America there would be nothing they could do. This seemed a sensible suggestion but it turned out to be impracticable. The Embassy will not issue visas to people who want to go to America to get married. There was no possibility of her going on a student's visa as she had not been accepted by any college. It was made very clear to us that if we were to go to America together at all we had to marry before we left Thailand.

The situation was further complicated by an acute shortage of money. I had not been receiving any salary. The money that had come out from the church groups and appeared on their books as salary had all gone into the day-to-day expenses of developing the village. I am a nonsmoker and a nondrinker, I had bought no clothes and possessed nothing. My expenses had been negligible, hence I had been able to put all the money that came from the U.S. into the village and into the small salaries of people who helped. By borrowing here and there I was able to get just enough money together to pay our fares: one ticket for me, one for Surin, and one for Ajana.

Our fears that Dr. Arie would stop the marriage were unfounded. The poor man did not get a chance. I was staying at the Railway Hotel in Bangkok and Ajana was with her uncle. We were married on May 31, 1960, by the Thai registrar of marriages in the presence of the American Vice Consul, who also issued a marriage certificate.

Because Ajana had been in America before, we had to obtain a clearance before the American Consul could issue a visa—although she was my legal wife. I was intensely worried about my mother so we decided that I should go home first and Ajana would join me as soon as her clearance came through. I left her with what I thought would be enough money and flew home. No sooner was I on the plane with Surin than Ajana's good friends and countrymen began working on her. Was she sure that the air ticket I had left her was a good one? She went along to the airline to check. Then, as the clearance still did not come, she began to run out of money. I had left her all I had but it was just not enough. When the clearance finally came she had to pawn some jewelry in order to pay the $25 fee for the visa.

When Surin and I arrived in America I was so broke I had to call my father collect to send some money so we could get on a bus for home. I had written to my father that I had married, so my family was reasonably informed.

Finally Ajana arrived. We began our married life in my parents' home, with no job and no prospects. I was given the impression by the church people that I had no right to be in America at all as I was supposed to be taking care of their major investment in leprosy work. I had thrown it all up, they implied, for some foreign woman who was probably no better than she ought to be. Some of the men and women connected with the church were very kind. Others needed to spend a little less time thinking about righteousness and more about being human.

We had not been home long before Ajana announced that she was pregnant. Thai women are proud of pregnancy and will announce conception at the earliest sign. This complicated our lives considerably and gave the neighbors plenty to occupy their minds.

My mother grew slowly worse until she fell into a coma. She had to be fed intravenously for several weeks before her death, and because Surin had such a soft loving manner and could handle the intravenous needles and tubes so skillfully our family doctor gave him wholehearted permission to nurse her. My gratitude to Surin was redoubled once again. In the funeral service our pastor made special mention of Surin's tender care. Mother had for years given her love and encouragement to my work in Thailand and now at the very end she was cared for by one of those she had helped. Surin stayed in America through Christmas and then returned to Thailand again to supervise our village and clinic.

Mother had died in August. In December Ajana had a miscarriage. In one way and another 1960 was not the kind of year I would like to go through again. Apart from these two heartbreaking events, we were very short of money. While the educated middle classes discussed the morality of my marrying a foreigner, giving her a child, leaving the jungle, and so on, the less-educated "tough" guys on the building sites made me welcome as a construction worker and put as much overtime in my way as possible so that I could get on my feet again financially. But I still had no definite plans for the future. Both Ajana and I wanted to go back to Thailand to continue the work, but I had had enough of existing on charity. I was now married and likely to have a family. If I returned to Thailand I would go only with a salary and a formal understanding that I had responsibilities. I felt that since the missionaries in Thailand are well paid and provided with good houses, there ought to be some place for me in such an organization if the work I had done and wanted to do was of any real value.

It was suggested that I should go to a seminary in St. Paul and become an ordained minister. This would entitle me to the usual minister's salary. This seemed a highly unworthy motive for becoming an ordained minister, however.

My motives for turning down this suggestion were, I think, respected, for a group of men from the church formed a committee to consider what to do with me. Eventually they offered me a salary of $300 a month if I would go back to Thailand. I agreed that this would be enough for Ajana and me to live on, but it would not be enough, by itself, to finance a new village. Trinity Village was almost complete. It needed only a little more attention. To start a new village, I would need money to buy land, tools, and other essential equipment. We talked the problem over and finally it was decided that I should go back to finish the work at Trinity. While I was so occupied efforts would be made to raise more money to start a new village. In a year's time we would all take stock of the situation and see how the future looked.

I must admit that I was not too happy about this vague arrangement. I agreed to it primarily for personal reasons. Ajana's mother had written a number of "all is forgiven" kind of letters and wanted us to live in Chiengmai. Also, I felt very bad about taking her daughter away without even being formally introduced. I wanted to make my peace with Ajana's family.

A month or so before we were due to leave I had trouble again from the amoebic dysentery. A fistula had developed in my intestine and had to be removed by surgery. A friend of mine, Dr. Ken Hodges, arranged some cut-price treatment for me in Minneapolis. Mrs. Hodges and Ajana had become good friends and one evening after I had been discharged from the hospital we were sitting in their house talking. One of their guests was Dr. A.

Henry Thompson from St. Peter, Minnesota. During the conversation Ken Hodges suggested to Dr. Thompson that I would be a good speaker for the St. Peter Lions Club. Immediately it was all arranged and shortly afterward I gave my talk. The St. Peter Lions Club group showed a great deal of interest in what I had to say and they arranged for me to meet a Lutheran pastor, the Reverend Millard Ahlstrom, who, they said, had very good political contacts.

I was later introduced to him and showed him my film. His immediate reaction was that my work would be of genuine interest to the people in Washington. To my surprise and awe, he just picked up the phone, dialed, and asked to speak to Senator Hubert Humphrey.

Senator Humphrey was out but the call was answered by Bill Connell, Humphrey's administrative assistant. Reverend Ahlstrom talked hard and fast with the result that Bill Connell agreed that if I went to Washington he would arrange for me to meet Senator Humphrey.

At this point Mr. Komatz, the owner of a construction company, offered to pay some of my expenses for a trip to Washington. He opened his wallet and brought out a fifty-dollar bill.

I hardly knew what to say. Everything was moving so fast. One of the things that really shook me, insignificant though it is, was that Mr. Komatz was a strong Republican while the Reverend Ahlstrom was an equally strong Democrat. Their political differences were thrust aside.

Ajana and I drove to Washington. On the morning of our appointment I read in the newspaper that Senator Humphrey was in Berlin. The skyscraper of hope I had been building began to crumble. It definitely teetered when I phoned Bill Connell. At first his secretary would not put me through to him. Then when I did finally get through he had forgotten all about me, and feeling a complete fool and a nuisance I reminded him about Reverend Ahlstrom and the telephone call. At this, the details seemed to click in place in Bill's mind, for he suggested I should come over to the Senate Office Building.

When Ajana and I arrived we were shown into Senator Humphrey's office and Bill Connell was there waiting for us. He seemed young and was clearly an active, dynamic kind of man. He asked me to tell him my story and show my slides. I launched into my story but it was difficult to put the story across well because every few minutes the phone would ring and Bill would have to drag his mind off to some other kind of business. I began to feel like a carpetbagger with my wares spread out on the living-room floor. "What," I asked myself, "am I doing here? What do I think all this is going to achieve?" Halfway through I felt like packing up my things and leaving, I was so convinced I was wasting everyone's time.

But I persevered and when I had finished, Bill said it was all very interesting and I was obviously on the level. Senator Humphrey had left instructions that if I did appear to have anything to offer, Bill was to work something out to assist me in developing my work.

Bill felt that the people I should see were those at the Peace Corps and on the Thai Desk in the State Department. An appointment was fixed for me with a staff member of the Peace Corps. We met the next day and he also showed interest. He had established himself as a minor expert on Thailand, having lived in Chiengmai for a few months and written a report on developing Thai culture. But at that time the Peace Corps was not very well organized and was looking for personnel rather than projects. It was soon clear that we could expect no more than best wishes from that quarter.

When we went to the Thai Desk at the State Department, Bill Connell turned up, too, and told them that Senator Humphrey thought they should listen carefully to what I had to say. By this time I realized that Bill was wholly sincere in wanting to help. He believed in the project and was not just doing a job.

The people on the Thai Desk gave me a pretty thorough interrogation. They wanted details. Vague generalities were not enough for them. Bill Connell, too, wanted to get something concrete worked out. He asked if it would be possible for my project to be sponsored by the U.S. Government in some way.

During the next few days we met so many people and did so much talking on and around the subject that it is all confused in my mind. The next great step forward was my meeting with Senator Humphrey. He returned from Berlin, held a press conference at the airport, came into his office, and there we were. He burst in and bustled around smiling and greeting everybody, had a five-minute conference with a reporter, and then had us shown into his office.

I was so nervous I could hardly talk and Ajana was so nervous she could hardly keep from crying. As exhibit specimens of leadership and adventurous spirit we must have made a poor showing.

Hubert Humphrey fortunately is a master at relaxing people. After listening to my halting speech for a few minutes he broke in and said, "My, you have a most attractive wife."

This compliment put Ajana completely at ease and she smiled a wonderful Thai smile. Although nobody had told me I was an attractive husband I felt better, too. Then Mr. Humphrey said that he was impressed by my project, that details could be gone into later, and that it might be a good idea if we all had our pictures taken. We did, and after much hand-shaking and expressions of mutual regard all around the interview came to an end.

The pleasure of meeting Senator Humphrey apart, the interview seemed to have accomplished absolutely nothing. But Bill Connell said that I should not worry as something would certainly be done.

And something was done. When we got back home there was a telegram from the State Department inviting me to go to Washington again, all expenses paid, to discuss the possibility of getting help for new villages from the United States Overseas Mission in

Thailand. There were more days of rather vague discussions, interviews with journalists, and then it was time for us to leave for Thailand. We had booked a berth on a Danish freighter several weeks before.

We had a long and interesting voyage back to Thailand, stopping at many ports of call along the way. Ajana was so overjoyed at not being seasick the first morning out that she celebrated by stuffing herself with Danish eclairs. This rich diet succeeded in bringing on the dreaded nausea and Ajana remained seasick for most of the voyage to Japan. We had a pleasant week in Japan while the ship was unloaded of cargo and were able to enjoy a honeymoon that we had lacked the time and money for a year earlier.

On the pier in Bangkok waiting to meet us stood Ajana's parents and my old friends Surin and Charn. Our welcome home was delightful in every way and we were in high spirits.

Chapter 7

My spirits were still high when I strode into the U.S.O.M. offices in Bangkok. In a matter of minutes they plummeted. I don't know what I had been expecting really, but it certainly wasn't the cool, disinterested response I got. I was told that there was little interest in wanting to squeeze another nuisance project into an already crowded schedule. It was nice meeting me, they said, and led me out the door.

I went up to Chiengdao very disheartened. Washington's promises were not, apparently, legal tender in Thailand. Month after month went by without a word. I wrote to Bill Connell and Senator Humphrey in Washington telling them about the attitude of the U.S. officials in Bangkok. No one had even been willing to come and look over my work. Finally, in December, I received a telegram from Bangkok asking me to report to U.S.O.M. as soon as possible. I wired that I would be down on the next train.

When I stepped off the train I was taken to a large air-conditioned car, driven to a hotel and registered, and then hustled to a meeting with all the local U.S.O.M. heads. With them was Dr. Fine of the State Department, who was in Thailand to check on a number of things. On his list was an instruction from Senator Humphrey to get some action on my case.

This meeting resulted in a proposal that I accept a job with U.S.O.M. in the community-development field. Bill Connell had warned me that I might be made such an offer. He had advised me to refuse it. His experience had taught him that when an agency doesn't know what to do with a man the easiest thing to do is to offer him a job. If he accepts he comes under normal service discipline and is promptly put to work someplace where he can do no harm or make a nuisance of himself. With Bill's words in mind I realized that once I went to work for U.S.O.M. my project could be shelved indefinitely while I obeyed orders and worked on "more urgent projects." If I refused I could be dismissed for insubordination.

After a lot of talking around the subject I got them to agree that if the Thai government requested a leprosy-rehabilitation project they would consider setting up the contract. Until such a request was made they could guarantee nothing.

While I was in Bangkok Ajana's family was having a reunion and my mother- and father-in-law were also in the city. By this time I was accepted by both of them and I had come to love and respect them very much. Dr. Arie had even begun to try to make a bridge player out of me. This was a compliment because bridge was his passion and he didn't choose his playing companions lightly. My mother-in-law, Charuey, was beginning to spoil me as her favorite son and even sided with me in family arguments.

When I discussed the result of the U.S.O.M. interview with Dr. Arie, he suggested that we should take steps to get the Thai government to request a program. He arranged for us to have an appointment with the Director General of Public Health in the Ministry of Health. For reasons I shall never fully understand, the Director General turned the idea down flat. He said his depart-ment already had excellent projects and there was no reason for them to request assistance in this field.

This was a bitter blow. It seemed that we had suddenly reached the end of the line. Ajana suggested that the idea had probably been turned down because I was not a doctor: medical people take a dim view of nonmedical people who engage in projects that are even only semimedical. The outlook was bleak. The church wouldn't help unless I became a minister; the Thai government wouldn't help because I was not a doctor; and U.S.O.M. wouldn't help because the Thai would not request it. I was so discouraged that I thought about taking any old job with U.S.O.M. just to raise enough money to get Ajana and me back home. Had it not been for the loyal support of my wife and her dear family I might very well have.

Dr. Arie came often to my village in Chiengdao. By this time he was its strongest supporter. He and I discussed what more could be done to help remove the social stigma attached to the village, and we came up with the idea of mixing leprosy cripples with ex-mental patients and other socially handicapped persons.

In February of 1962 an old school chum of Dr. Arie's, the Director General of Public Welfare, Mr. Pakorn Angsusingha, came to Chiengmai on a visit. Dr. Arie decided to risk another rebuff from the Thai government and invited Mr. Pakorn to visit our village. Briefly, he came, he saw and was conquered. He told me our village was more prosperous than any of the villages developed by his department and that he was sure our approach to the problem of rehabilitating leprosy patients was sound and realistic. He decided then and there to make a request to U.S.O.M. for assistance from the American foreign-aid program.

At last the bureaucratic machinery began to turn and it was agreed that U.S.O.M. would finance the establishment and development of two new villages which were to be completely self-supporting in two years. The grant was for $20,000 a year, or $40,000 in all. This sum was to cover everything, including salaries for myself and four Thai assistants, operating expenses, and two new jeeps. My own standing would be as a private contractor engaged by U.S.O.M. to do a specific job of work. I would not be an employee.

I was richly rewarded by the help, friendliness, and enthusiasm of the Thai Public Welfare Department. Mr. Pakorn got the scheme off the ground and then, when he was promoted into the Ministry of Internal Development, his successor, Mr. Suwan Ruenyote, carried on. Both men have high ideals and a sincere desire to help the poor of their own country, and they are unfortunately handicapped by small budgets. Most of the money available for government spending necessarily goes to defense, education, and communications development. Public welfare is very much a Cinderella ministry and needs all the assistance it can get. The department is given most of the unpleasant and difficult problems—from aiding unemployed and resettling refugees to providing cheap rental apartments, rehabilitating prostitutes, caring for flood victims and orphans, and coordinating religious, social, and educational organizations. To my mind a public-welfare program is not only necessary sociologically, it is right politically. Communism cannot be defeated by weapons alone: only increased education, health, and public-welfare services can finally win the battle against the Communists' propaganda.

I signed the joint contract with U.S.O.M. and the Thailand Department of Public Welfare on June 15, 1962, and immediately hired Surin and his brother Charn. Dr. Wong and Dr. Arunee, who had been with us at Chiengdao, had eventually tired of the jungle clinic and were disinclined to live with more inconveniences which would undoubtedly arise in the new projects. Therefore, much to our sorrow, they moved in January of 1963 to Arunee's home town of Payao and set up a clinic there with Arunee's physician brother. Our villagers were saddened to see the only doctors in the district move away. Before we had left the United States I had optimistically encouraged Paul Larson to come to Thailand again to help with the expected contract project, and I'd met and encouraged a young North Dakota lad, Paul Sletten, to come also. Both fellows arrived during the period while I was still trying to get things worked out and so they had moved into our Chiengdao village to work while we waited. Paul Larson was receiving a small allowance for his expenses from his home church.

In May Paul Sletten had to return to the U.S. to continue his college studies and so he missed our contract projects. However, he continued to be keenly interested in what we were doing and was instrumental in 1964 in persuading the Lions Club of Fargo, North Dakota, to send our villagers enough money to purchase a small farm tractor. This was a great contribution to our work.

The first step to establishing the new villages was to select the land sites. The contract ensured that the Thai government would provide land, but we were going to have to search out potential areas and clear the title through the local officials. We had agreed to use virgin land if possible because we did not want the government to confiscate land that was already in use.

Though our orders for the two jeeps had been given special A.I.D. priority, we were shocked to learn they wouldn't arrive for at least six months. Instead of dashing off to look for our new land, we chugged along uncertainly in our old jeep truck now running on its twentieth spring leaf. Its engine could only be described as an uneasy alliance of Japanese and European repair parts tenuously clinging to an American block. Whenever we set off to explore some new area we literally didn't know when and how we would return.

We began narrowing our search to two areas. One was along the Lee River in the Lee district of Lampoon Province south of Chiengmai. This valley provided the only pass through the mountains from Chiengmai to Bangkok and we had watched the road gradually improve from a very temporary and treacherous trail in 1952 to a rather heavily traveled graded road in 1962. The area was being developed quite rapidly now by refugees from the area newly flooded by the Phumiphol Dam on the Ping River to the west, but there was still land available for our purposes if we could but find it.

The other area was along the new road still under construction from Haut District in Southern Chiengmai Province connecting over the mountain to the Maesareang District of Maehongsong Province. This was to be the first all-weather road to connect Maehongsong Province with the rest of Thailand. The road crossed mountain ridges inhabited only by mountain tribal people and so it seemed a likely area for us to develop a new village site.

We found a promising location in Haut District along the Jam River and hopefully began clearing land. However, the district officer felt uneasy about the prospect of leprosy patients living upstream from him and he refused us use of the land.

So we investigated another area in Hangdong District just south of Chiengmai. We used a work crew of mental patients from Suanprung Hospital to help clear aisles through the jungle growth so the land could be surveyed and mapped. It was the rainy season again and work was wet, slippery, and exhausting. We also had to watch that we did not lose any of the patients as they had a tendency to forget their purpose and wander off. Once two patients were gone for four days before they strolled back into Chiengmai. Our formal request for the land got stalled somewhere in the government mill, and it eventually became apparent we wouldn't be able to use this land within our contract time.

Several other promising locations had been discovered by our fellows in the Lee District but we seemed always to run into some problem. And so after three months of our two-year contract time we were still without land to work and still without the new jeeps. After the years that Surin and I had spent grubbing out the village in Chiengdao without definite financial support or without any equipment, we had jestingly referred to village construction under an A.I.D.-Thai Public Welfare contract as a "soft touch" and "a sure thing." By this time it no longer seemed so soft or so sure.

We received a further blow when we got word that Paul Larson had lost his church support. Our budget was too small to allow us to care adequately for Paul. We all knew he would have to have a better situation as it was unfair to him to have him labor on with such little reward.

Bill Connell came to the rescue again and helped arrange for Paul to enter the Peace Corps. The Corps' regulations require that all Volunteers must successfully complete a period of training and selection, and so Paul had to fly to a training program in Hawaii to see if he could qualify to return to Thailand. He ultimately completed his training and was sent officially as a Peace Corps Volunteer to Thailand. He was not allowed to return with us, however, but spent a successful two years in a Public Welfare settlement in Takli District of Nakornsawan Province. In 1965 Paul was given a position as a regional A.I.D. officer in Laos and did an outstanding job. We were happy to see Paul succeed so well, but we were all a bit sad to see him leave our work.

Though we didn't get Paul we were compensated by having Charlie Cobb of the Peace Corps. Charlie had come to Thailand with the first group of Peace Corps Volunteers. He was teaching in Chiengmai and took an interest in our project. He began working with us on weekends and in a few months he was transferred to working with us full time.

When we were offered a new piece of land in the Haut District we rushed to see it. It was on the mountain ridge of Bao Kao along the Maesareang road at about the thirty-six-and-a-half-kilometer marker. The land had a gentle slope and the mountain view was superb. The soil was thin, and it was questionable whether the springs could provide enough water for the dry season. The mountain folk (all Loowah tribes) were not overjoyed to see leprosy cripples and mental patients moving in. They soon became accustomed to our collection, however, and we all got along quite well together.

With our Haut District village underway we now turned again to the Lee District to find a location for the second village. We stopped in to describe our plans once again to the governor of Lampoon. The governor had become quite interested in our project and now suggested that we be given a tract of land under the control of the Land Department. This area was about seven and a half kilometers north of Lee Village and was located on the far side of the Lee River which at this point came nearly to the Chiengmai–Bangkok road. All that needed doing was to construct a bridge over the river and extend a road a half a mile or so and we'd have a very convenient location. On February 1 we moved in the first group of leprosy cripples; they were sent by the Lampang Leprosy Foundation. The grapevine communication system saw to it that a steady stream of new residents kept coming. Thus, seven months after the start of our contract project we had two village sites and a population at Lee of thirty, and at Haut of twenty-five. All we had to do now was to turn these cripples and beggars into self-supporting citizens.

Some "professional" patients came to our villages merely to see what handouts were available. When they found out they would have to learn how to work, many of them left. We never made any pretext of supplying a lot of material charity. We provided all the tools a man could demonstrate he could use, usually a hoe and a knife and sometimes an ax. Few people knew how to use any tools other than these. We always provided all the seeds a man could plant, after he had prepared the soil. Anyone could claim as much land as he could conceivably use; there were no limits on the amount. We gave temporary permission the first year and made the land allocation permanent the following year if his industry warranted it. We found this system an extremely effective stimulus.

Despite the opportunities that beckoned, some of the patients required large doses of persuasion. I remember one patient; I'll call him S. He was twenty-five years old and had never worked for a living. He had contracted leprosy as a boy and spent his youth begging in markets. When he was twenty he wandered into a leprosy mission and received DDS therapy at the clinic. When he reached twenty-five he was declared negative and discharged from the mission clinic. For a short time he dreamed of a normal life in his old home town, but his scars and disfigurement prevented him from being accepted, and he presented himself at our village.

He was given a piece of land, seeds to plant, tools, rice to eat, and a temporary house until he could build one for himself. He was now free from persecution and ridicule, though he was no longer free from work.

The first few days were very difficult for him. His body ached from the strain of unaccustomed exercise, his hands blistered and cracked, and the sun beat down on his head and back. He scratched himself on some sharp thorns and his arms itched after contact with some poisonous weeds.

At night he began to question his decision to come to the village. What was the point of it all? He thought back to his begging days when in the cool of the shade in the market all he had to do was to hold out his bowl and wait for enough money to buy a dish of noodles. Then, with a full stomach, he could return to the shade and sleep for a few hours.

S. considered the possibility of returning to begging but decided that if he played his cards well he might be able to lead an equally easy life in the village. He went to discuss his plight with the superintendent.

Drawing on all his experience as a professional beggar, he pleaded his case. The work was too hard for him. He had a poor life and was weak and unfit for hard labor. If the superintendent was really sincere he would realize that S. needed help. He needed more food and more clothing. He also needed someone to help him clear his land and build his house. It just wasn't fair to expect a poor leprosy patient to do everything for himself. And if, S. suggested, the superintendent refused to help him, then S. promised that there would be trouble. It wasn't right to see all these poor people working so hard and he, S. would point out to them

197

what was wrong with the organization and they would all leave and the superintendent would have no village.

Patiently the superintendent listened to S.'s complaints. Then he put the situation to S. this way:

"Well, S., you're a free man and if you want to leave you can. You can take a few of your friends with you if you like, but I doubt if they'll come."

"You don't give me enough. Why should I stay?"

"What do you want?"

"Well, I don't know. More clothes for a start."

"I'd have thought land was worth more than a few old clothes. Think about that piece of land you're working on. It will all be yours very soon, if you work it well. The soil is good and it's next to the river. What do you think it's worth?"

"I don't know. Six thousand *baht*, perhaps."

"Yes, that's about right. Has anyone ever offered you six thousand *baht* before?"

"No."

"Well, then, what are you complaining about? Many Thai farmers would like that piece of land, S. And remember, we give you all the seeds you need, and some tools, and rice to eat until you can grow or buy your own. All we ask you to do is to plant the seeds and look after them."

"It's hard work."

"Of course it is. But if everybody else works for his land why shouldn't you? You're no worse off than many of the others. Better off than many because you're younger. Tell me, how much would you save after a day's begging when you've eaten and shared with the other beggars?"

"It depends. Sometimes three or even five *baht*. Sometimes nothing. But begging is easy, isn't it?"

"Let's say five *baht* a day. In one year with luck you can save fifteen hundred *baht*. In four years you can save six thousand *baht*. Have you ever saved any money, by the way?"

"No."

"Never mind, let's pretend that you are able to save. It would take you four years to save six thousand *baht*. If you stay here and work your land you get not only the land worth six thousand *baht* but the security that comes from knowing that every year that land is going to produce for you and that nobody can ever take it away from you. After a little effort you've got land, crops, and a house."

"I suppose you're right."

"You can prove whether I'm right very quickly, can't you?"

"Yes. O.K., I'll try—but it's hard work."

S. tried again and did succeed. Others refused to try and left the villages but they were few in number. Most of the people who came needed little persuasion and often those who left returned later when they saw how well the village was developing. They were made welcome on the same terms as before.

Our villages had barely begun functioning when both faced serious water problems: one arising from too much water and the other from too little. In the Haut village we ran so short of water we weren't able to irrigate the gardens. Acharn Gon Ratanasaka, who was the head of the Maesareang road construction company working in the vicinity, heard of our plight and immediately offered a solution. As the road construction progressed, his workers set up temporary villages along the way. They were now in a lovely little valley near the fifty-five-kilometer marker near Gong Loy but would soon move on to a new location at about the eighty-kilometer point. Acharn Gon suggested we move our entire village onto the fifty-five-kilometer site and he provided his trucks to move us. What a tremendous help this was! The new location had a small stream and rich fertile soil and even a few fruit trees the construction company had set in. Our people were delighted with their new homes and they were all moved in by May of 1963.

The other village in Lee District was in danger of being cut off when the rains came. Unless we built a bridge across the river we wouldn't be able to cross it in floodtime. We put Charlie Cobb, the Peace Corps Volunteer, in charge of investigating what we could do.

Charlie had an engineering degree although not in civil engineering or construction. After conferring with Thai civil engineers in the Highway Department and after drawing up some construction plans with Manley Irish, Charlie decided that we could build the bridge ourselves. Manley Irish, a Peace Corps training dropout who had come to Thailand on his own, was an engineer also, with a wealth of practical experience. He unfortunately returned to America before we started on the bridge.

Next Charlie got in touch with the Peace Corps officials in Bangkok and arranged for a group of husky Volunteers to spend their school teaching vacations with us building a bridge. We soon had Peace Corps Volunteers Ed Clark, Ron Vanderklok, Steve Anders, Homer Brawley, and Richard Kleeman on the site with Charlie.

The river was fifty yards across and the span would have to be twenty feet above it in order to survive the flood crests. The fellows pitched in undaunted, however, and began digging for the bridge footings. Their enthusiasm was quickly dashed by the swirling water and sand. As fast as they could make an excavation it filled with sand and water. After a month of strenuous physical exertion but with practically no visible accomplishment the fellows gave it all up as an impossible job and left. We felt grateful to them for all their efforts. Though the Peace Corps later wrote up the experience as a failure for summertime vacation projects I feel that it was a worthwhile learning experience for the fellows. All but one of them returned a year later to see our bridge standing.

After the Peace Corps fellows left we turned to A.I.D. for advice. Officials there told me we could probably build the bridge for about $20,000. They didn't tell me where I could find $20,000.

Finally Surin located an old Thai gentleman, Cuan Chisawat, who had years of experience building wooden bridges in the area. He said he would supervise our job if we arranged with the Highway Department to borrow their two-ton pile-driver hammer. The Department not only loaned us the hammer but delivered it in their truck along with the hand winch and cable. The old gentleman then constructed his own flimsy scaffold and frame to operate the hammer. Seeing that two-ton hunk of steel being cranked up and down on the spindly teakwood frame was enough to send anyone running for cover. And yet the old man drove down those twenty-five-foot teak logs as easily as could be. We had had the logs ready for him because the governor had given us permission to cut them. A couple of locally recruited elephants dragged the logs to the bridge site. Soon also the local people began to volunteer their labor. In no time we had a real construction project going, and at practically no cost.

As the bridge gradually took shape and the neighboring citizens saw that it would soon be a reality, the feeling toward our villagers changed markedly. The bridge would of course be as useful to them as to us. Any feelings of doubt or hostility which may have been felt earlier were dissolved in gratitude for the bridge. From this time on there was never anything but cooperation between our villagers and the neighbors, and the children from our leprosy families were readily accepted in the local Huey Han village school.

The bridge was completed in three months. On August 9, 1963, during the middle of the rainy season, Mr. Manit Bhuranaphan, governor of Lampoon, and Steve Dobrenchuk, the U.S. Consul in Chiengmai, came down for a special bridge-opening ceremony. They were joined by all of the lesser local officials, plus twenty Buddhist priests and several hundred villagers. It was a gala day marred for me only by the nervousness I felt whenever I looked at the rising crest of the river. Would it be too much for our bridge? Would the bridge hold through the ceremonies?

Actually my fears were groundless: the bridge was as sturdy as steel. Later, when flood torrents caught up tons of floating stumps and trees and hurled them against the bridge in savage fury, hundreds of area residents turned out to break up the log jams and keep the bridge free. They continue to this day to protect their bridge whenever it is in jeopardy. For a total cost of less than $900 (mostly for steel bolts) we spanned that river and cemented relations for all time with the local people.

Once the bridge at Lee was finished and after our Haut village was moved to Gong Loy, we were able to concentrate on helping the people learn to become self-supporting. Since we had used up nearly a year in getting settled, the Thai Department of Public Welfare requested A.I.D. to give us an additional year of assistance. A.I.D. extended the contract another year and thus gave us the time and funds we needed to build the villages to the extent originally envisaged.

Mr. Pakorn Angsusingha, the Director General, felt as I do, that in addition to the incalculable gain to the afflicted individual, rehabilitating disabled people (changing them from parasites to producers) affords a nation a considerable economic advantage. Soon after he had seen our Chiengdao village he had suggested that we establish a foundation to continue our work and we began to set one up. By the time we had taken care of all the legal procedures Mr. Pakorn had moved up to the Ministry of Internal Development and Mr. Suwan Ruenyote had replaced him as Director General. Mr. Suwan was if anything even more enthusiastic and helpful and came to Chiengmai and Lampoon to visit our villages in 1964. By then our New Life Foundation to help rehabilitate socially handicapped persons in Thailand was a reality.

Many Thai citizens helped in setting up the Foundation but the work rested heavily on the shoulders of the eight Thai who together with myself make up the acting committee. My father-in-law, Dr. Arie Watana, was eager to take a part as was another doctor from Suanprung, Dr. Khanan. The committee could not have functioned without my old friend and assistant Surin Chowapisit; Surin still does most of the leg work. Acharn Gon of the Maesareang road construction organization willingly agreed to become a member, as did the Chiengmai Public Health Officer, Dr. Ahmon. Three outstanding ladies also accepted service on the committee: Mrs. Buphon Nemmanhaemenda, a leader in Thai social welfare circles and a sister-in-law of the present Thai ambassador to the U.S.; Mrs. Phun Ahsasongcram, active in many Chiengmai business and social activities; and Mrs. Wittayasai, who replaced her late husband, a regional judge, on the original committee.

Princess Prem Bhurachart and General Luang Kampanartsayakorn, who are very well known in Thailand, have given us gracious assistance from time to time.

In April of 1965 I was asked to represent our New Life Foundation at the National Council of Social Welfare convention in Bangkok. I had presented an exhibit of our work in Trinity Village at the council's conference three years earlier. Thailand's lovely Queen Sirikit attended both conferences, and each time I was privileged to be presented to her and had a chance to tell her personally about our work. This time, as I stood waiting for her and Prime Minister Thanom Kittakachorn to arrive at our exhibit, my mind played over the first meeting and the embarrassment I had suffered. I had been told but ten minutes before their arrival that their Majesties, the King and Queen, were coming with the Prime Minister to open the conference and that I was supposed to stand next to our display and explain the pictures to them. I was so surprised I couldn't think of what to do. All sorts of questions bombarded my mind. How do you address royalty? Do you bow or salute or kneel or what? This was a subject never covered in my education and my knees began to knock. A Thai standing nearby sensed my consternation and said, "Don't worry, just talk in English."

"Talk what?" I gasped.

And then the royal party was standing before me and I heard my voice wavering somewhere far off. The Queen, being truly a queen, gave a kindly smile, stepped forward and began quietly to speak to me. Her charming manner dissolved my nervousness and I shook her offered hand in gratitude. I shall always be her fervent admirer.

Their Majesties made another visit to the Chiengdao District in January 1965. They came to visit the ancient royal campsite in Muang Ih, and this time we were fully ready for the occasion. All of our villagers were gathered around our gaily decorated village driveway waiting for their Majesties to pass by. As the royal car pulled to a stop I stepped forward and presented his Majesty the King a life-sized teakwood deer made especially for him by our carvers. The sight seemed to please him and he chatted for some time with the villagers. They were thrilled almost speechless.

Although I had now visited with the Queen twice before and seen her from a distance several different times, I still felt a bit dizzy and frightened when we shook hands again at the convention. Here was I, a small-town boy from Minnesota, standing before the Queen of Thailand and she was nodding appreciatively at the pictures of our villages. I couldn't help feeling a little bit proud of the success of my work.

There had been other gratifying recognition too. The Public Welfare Department had sponsored my film of the villages on Bangkok Sunday afternoon television. We had been invited to present our rehabilitation work to the Thailand National Medical Convention in 1964, and the doctors had shown much interest. Articles had been printed in Thai newspapers and both the Public Health and the Public Welfare journals.

The main points about our New Life Foundation we tried to get across in all the articles, talks, or films ran like this:

1 People must be made to face their own problems. They must realize that if they have not sufficient food, they may be partly to blame. The world owes no one a living for doing nothing.

2 By mixing people handicapped different ways it becomes difficult to label the communities, and the social stigma of "a leper village" disappears fairly quickly. Also, people with different handicaps can be of more help to one another. Crippled ex-leprosy patients, for example, help ex-mental patients by supervising projects and giving enthusiastic drive and incentive to group projects. The ex-mental patients, generally steady, plodding workers, help the ex-leprosy patients with their physical strength and undamaged hands and feet.

3 No man is granted title to his land until he has earned it. The Foundation is not an almsgiving organization and it expects the people in its villages to do their best to deserve the gift of a piece of land.

4 Free rice—usually six liters a week per person—is discontinued after the first successful crop. (Usually within one year)

5 The people must build their own houses. Only thatch is provided by the Foundation.

6 The people are expected to work together to build the necessary roads, bridges, and irrigation ditches. This follows local custom in most rural areas.

7 Only a single set of hand tools is presented to each man, although if someone can produce evidence that he has a special skill requiring other tools or equipment (for example, charcoal making) the Foundation will provide what is required. General rules are always subject to adjustment since we treat each patient as an individual.

8 No limit is placed on the free distribution of seeds, provided they are properly planted and the shoots tended.

9 The Foundation tries to assist individuals on the basis of their own ability and ambition. Equal assistance for all has not been found suitable in work of this kind.

10 At first the villages tend to develop on communal lines, mainly because the people crave security. Soon, however, as the village becomes more prosperous individual enterprise becomes more common. When the villages are fully developed the people lose nearly all desire for socialistic living.

All of the more than two hundred persons who had taken up new lives in our Foundation's villages at Lee and Haut were completely self-supporting well before the end of our contract time. At Lee we had dispensed rice for only ten months before the villagers were able to provide their own. At both villages they had enjoyed several bountiful harvests of corn, soybeans, peanuts, garlic, onions, and truck-garden vegetables. Acharn Gon, the head of the construction company who had given us the site at Lee, had also supplied some cattle, so that the villagers were raising cows in addition to chickens, rabbits, and fish. Their fruit orchards and strawberry beds stretched handsomely across the valleys, interlaced in pleasing patterns with new irrigation ditches and roads. They experimented so successfully with new crops and different ways of doing things that they inspired their unafflicted neighbors to improve their farming methods. Our sweet corn made a big hit in the local market, and one widow lady grew popcorn that popped. A group of the villagers started a successful charcoal business, and several mental patients set up a weaving industry to provide baskets for the charcoal makers.

Many of our ex-leprosy patients, such as Jumnean, our champion potato grower, employed other leprosy and mental patients. Badly crippled Jumnean brought in three thousand *baht* on one potato crop alone. The average yearly income for a farm family in North Thailand is about fifteen hundred *baht* (around $75).

This affluence, I have to admit, was not without its complications. The settlers at Trinity, our very first village at Chiengdao, by now had become so well off that their village was a "must" on the list of every itinerant gambler and fighting-cock manager. For the most part our people resisted the lures and vices, I'm happy to say. Having come so far they did not want to squander their money or do anything else that might jeopardize their new life.

As important as their economic independence was (it certainly was a basic, contributing factor) I don't believe that for any one of them it meant as much as their social acceptance in the neighboring villages. Our people were allowed to move in and out of the markets in the other villages. Several of our ex-leprosy carpenters were hired out to build houses. Our villagers' children were welcome in the outside schools, and one township hired our carpenters to build its school furniture. Many of the unmarried patients gained normal wives who moved into our villages. And more than ten unafflicted families have moved into each of our three villages.

By June 14, 1965, when our contract expired, I felt it was time for me to get away for a while. I needed a rest and it was a good idea to demonstrate that our folks could continue to support themselves without a foreigner looking on. There were now more than eight hundred persons in the three villages. Additionally, Ajana and I wanted to visit America and give our little sons, Timmy and Danny, a chance to see my family and friends there.

It was not easy to think of leaving. It became almost unbearable when we said our final farewell that humid afternoon in June at the Chiengmai railroad station. Had Ajana's sister and mother not tried so valiantly to hide their tears, I might better have been able to give voice to some of my feelings. I was almost too choked to smile, let alone speak. What wonderful people are the Thai!

Abruptly the train whistled and it began to roll, carrying us forward to what lay ahead. What does lie ahead? How can I continue to serve my country and my Thailand? May God continue to guide my way.

PRICE 6 12.45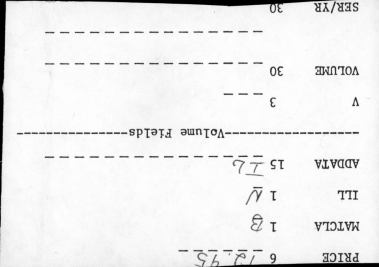

MATCLA 1 ℬ

ILL 1 𝑁

ADDATA 15 𝐼𝑇𝑏

------------------------Volume Fields--------------------

V 3

VOLUME 30

SER/YR 30

B
W 1961

Leprosy Thailand

ANALYSIS OF LEPROSY CONTROL METHODS

RICHARD S. BUKER M.D., M.P.H., DR.P.H.

Advisor in Leprosy to Protestant Missions
in Thailand, Vietnam, and Laos
Supported by the American Leprosy Missions, Inc.
297 Park Avenue South, New York 10, N.Y.
Digested in *The Journal of the American Medical Association*,
VOL. 193, NO. 8, August 23, 1965

Introduction: The complete Leprosy Program is made up of four divisions. Rarely are all four divisions found in one area. Various groups attempt special phases of the total program depending on their vision, finances, and opportunities. The complete program may be outlined as follows:

I. *Survey* of the total population, recording the name and addresses with an examination of 95 to 98 per cent of all leprosy patients. Records of the contacts of patients are made.

II. *Treatment* of 70 to 80 per cent of all patients recorded for five to twenty years. To do this one must start treating some 95 per cent of all known patients. For the majority of patients nothing further will be needed.

III. *Hospitalization.* Ten to 20 per cent of all patients will need hospitalization for something during their sickness. Fifty per cent of those hospitalized will be for ulcers. Forty per cent will need hospitalization for reconstructive surgery. The remaining 10 per cent will require drug stabilization or treatment for reactions or intercurrent medical and surgical conditions. These percentages are all relative and vary from time to time and place to place.

209

IV. *Rehabilitation*. Many leprosy patients need to be rehabilitated. This is particularly true of those who have to go to the hospital. Inoperable cripples are especially in need of rehabilitation. Many able-bodied leprosy patients because of the social stigma also need help. Vocational training has an important place in this program. Some will be rehabilitated in their own homes, some in special sheltered industries or cooperative ventures and some in self-help villages established with the needs of leprosy people in mind.

It is obvious that whatever part of the Leprosy Program one decides to do, a clear policy of what is being attempted and why is indicated. Dr. Price has emphasized this need. In his summary he says, "The main needs are for: the control and treatment of the early case, the rehabilitation of the partially disabled, and the care of the totally disabled." To those who have as a goal "the eradication of leprosy" one wonders just what part of this program is important—what are the weak places and where should the future program lead us? It is the purpose of this paper to analyze the various control methods of importance which have been tried in the past and to note the important features of each.

Leprosy Control Before 1900

The classic example of near eradication of leprosy in the past has been the near disappearance of leprosy in Central Europe during the middle centuries of this era. There was no ability at early diagnosis, there was no effective treatment and yet it disappeared. There was a definite attempt at isolation but for a long time this certainly had no influence on the total number of cases. What then was the factor that resulted in this near eradication? It is generally conceded that the raising of living standards produced the factors which resulted in the change. But just what in these standards was the factor that was most important? Many theories have been advanced. M. Oberdoerffer in a paper read before the Far Eastern Association of Tropical Medicine in Hanoi, 1938, suggested that the common corn cockle, *Agrostemma githago*, was often mixed with poorly cleaned corn. Ergot was sometimes mixed with other grains. Both of these contain a sapotoxin which is injurious to the adrenals. The elimination of this sapotoxin by better methods of cleaning grains may have influenced the decrease in the number of leprosy cases. The Oberdoerffer views of the importance of the sapotoxins in *colocasia alocasia* and *xanthosoma* as a factor in leprosy epidemiology are strongly opposed by many; the fact remains that those countries which use *colocasia* or taro as a food do have a lot of leprosy. It is probably true, we may never know all the factors which contributed to the decrease of leprosy in Europe.

1900–50 *Methods of Dealing with Leprosy*

For many years a leprosy colony or sanatorium or home was considered the logical approach for getting rid of leprosy in a given area. This seemed logical. Here was a contagious disease, the natural thing to do was to isolate the cases and the disease would disappear. Unfortunately the majority of government officials still have this limited and unscientific view of leprosy. Perhaps the classical example which really disproved its value was the trial in the Philippine Islands. This area was not so large but that reasonable observations and conclusions could be drawn. A law was enacted that *all* leprosy cases should be removed to Culion Island well isolated from the rest of the islands. Cases could not swim back to their homes and clandestine shipping could be fairly well controlled. The finances were assured by the American Government. The U.S. Public Health Service provided needed medical supervision. After over ten years of trial it was realized that the plan was a failure so far as eradicating leprosy from the Philippines. Every year there was approximately the same number of new cases being found and sent to Culion. Two important factors made the scheme impossible. The first is the long time which leprosy takes to develop in a given case before it can be recognized; the latter part of this period may, many times, be infectious. The second factor is human nature—no one is going to submit to being transported from home, loved ones, familiar surroundings to an outcast life among the forsaken ones. Only as the law descends upon them and forces this issue will they go. In the meantime most cases will have become contagious and one or more susceptible persons infected. This is what happened in the Philippines. The present much-changed control program in the Philippines is meeting the need according to the best-understood methods.

Our own experience in Kengtung, Burma, on a much smaller scale was very impressive. From 1928 to 1933 we established a permanent colony supposing we were doing the most modern and effective thing possible. Little by little the truth dawned upon us that what we were doing against leprosy per se was practically nothing. We had one hundred cases of leprosy in a well-organized colony. As we made sample surveys of the entire state, we realized there must be some ten thousand cases in all. What was the value of spending all this time and energy on one hundred when ninety-nine hundred or more were at large? Different methods were necessary and toward that end we began to develop other ways of reaching out to the greater numbers. As is usually the case in all missionary-attempted schemes, ideas run far ahead of finances. Later in this article our detailed plans will be discussed. From the above discussion we would not conclude that colonies have no place in leprosy control programs. There is a place for them but because of their extreme per capita expense, their psychological unattractiveness to the patient, they must be carefully integrated into a total plan. As few as possible should be maintained, doing the things that only a colony can do; those which offer primarily a place to live for able-bodied leprosy patients should be abandoned. The colony is a place for research. The colony is a place where acutely ill patients or those needing surgery are accepted for limited periods of time only. Every patient who comes to a colony should realize that the probable time of his departure is determined the day he arrives. Places for the totally crippled should be a part of the program of the Public Welfare Department. These cripples are not a public-health problem. Colonies may well be the center from which active control work branches out to all parts of the region needing leprosy eradication. We must realize, as Dr. Robert Cochrane says, that "eradication of leprosy cannot be done in isolation."

Factors Which Influence the Spread of Leprosy

There are certain factors which influence the spread of leprosy. These factors aid us in the basic approach. As mentioned by Chandy and others, "It is generally believed that children are more susceptible to leprosy infections than adults. Our observations at Faizabad and Barabanki as reported do not lend support to this view." Dr. T. F. Davey from his Nigerian work says, concerning childhood leprosy, "With many early cases among adults it is clearly indicated that susceptibility to infection was not confined to childhood and youth." Dr. Badger in his chapter on epidemiology in Dr. Cochrane's book says, "Analysis of the available information suggests that the age at infection is dependent on the age at contact and the intimacy of contact rather than the greater susceptibility of the disease of any particular age group." On the same page Dr. Cochrane notes, "This, therefore is further evidence of the importance of the statement that it is clearly intimacy of contact that determines the susceptibility of the person and that age may be a less important factor than hitherto suspected." Our own observations in Thailand and Burma are that over one half of our leprosy cases developed clinical leprosy after the age of twenty and many after thirty-five years of age.

The matter of lepromatous cases with high bacterial index being the main source of infection for new cases can be seriously questioned. This and the importance of long and close contact were assumed to be the most important factors in the spread of leprosy to new cases. Over one half of the cases in our leprosy clinics in Thailand had no close relative and had no knowledge of contact with another case of leprosy. Certainly these people would have recognized a lepromatous case of leprosy, for leprosy is well known in these areas. Another factor which needs clarification, if the above factors influencing the spread of leprosy are true, is, why are there so many nonleprosy cases in homes where one or at most two lepromatous cases lived? It seems true that infectivity is often not proportional to the number of bacilli being given off by the infective patient. To study these problems we must leave the colony and continue to gather information in the villages and homes of the patients. An integrated health program will probably reveal important facts. Genetics and immunity hold some important answers which we need to know.

Treatment Clinics

The next method of control that we will review are clinics for leprosy patients. We are particularly interested in the relatively large areas where treatment control clinics are conducted such as are found in India, Nigeria, and Thailand. It is true that any program to eradicate leprosy must have been underway over five years, better fifteen years, before its true value can be ascertained. In India and Nigeria these plans have been functioning on sufficiently large scale and long enough to give us some answers. In Thailand the plan has now been functioning eight years and certain things are observable. With the advent of the sulfone drugs a reliable, easily dispensed, and relatively cheap drug became available. This drug has made large-scale treatment possible with much greater success than in the presulfone days.

In order to really know the value of Treatment Control Centers (now often called SET—Survey Educational Treatment programs) a carefully planned trial was outlined by Dr. R. V. Wardekar of India. The trial, in order to be of real value, covered several centers to minimize individual variations and that conclusions might be drawn which are general enough to apply to all areas. The facts recorded have covered ten or more years. He was not hindered by the various changing concepts of a political control. As the years go by he has recorded facts of great value. The nature of his work is shown by quotations from his Fourth Report. "PURPOSE A control unit is a field experiment to find out whether leprosy can be controlled through a planned use of DDS and whether there are other incidental advantages of such an approach.

"WORK OF THE UNIT Each unit covers a population of about twenty-five thousand. Every year intensive survey work is done. It has not been possible to do any village or other segregation of infectious cases. Even experimental work in Kerala was not successful as far as segregation was concerned. Cases are detected and each case is persuaded to take treatment. Along with surveys, leprosy education is also done.

"PROGRESS OF THE WORK Unit heads had not only the human and sympathetic outlook but the necessary academic qualifications and a scientific disposition of mind. It may be mentioned here that the control unit differs in one respect. In control work it is the worker who has to go after the patients while in other antileprosy work the patients on their own come for treatment. The reversal of the role between the worker and the patient creates innumerable difficulties. As this type of field work is a fight against lethargy and prejudices of the people, the workers have to be well conversant with the psychology of the patients and also realize their economic and other difficulties. There are thus innumerable obstacles at every step and workers sometimes get disheartened, particularly when patients become irregular or when the community does not cooperate at the time of the surveys. These experiences are very trying and have to be faced very patiently.

"DATA The purpose of this work is to find out whether leprosy is controlled after working in an area for ten to fifteen years."

Toward this end ten control units were established in different parts of India. Perhaps the most important fact which can be assessed and reported on over the years is the percentage of deformities in the new cases registered each year. Reports on this for seven years were available in 1961.

1st year	28.1 per cent of cases had deformities.
2nd year	18.4 per cent of cases had deformities.
3rd year	10.3 per cent of cases had deformities.
4th year	7.0 per cent of cases had deformities.

5th year   10.5 per cent of cases had deformities. A different and
    better approach was made in the survey work.
6th year   7.3 per cent of cases had deformities.
7th year   6.3 per cent of cases had deformities.

From the work so far done there is evidence that when control work
is done with vigor and care, good results are obtained.

The Treatment Control Centers of Nigeria are really based upon
some twenty years of excellent planning by several experienced lep-
rologists before the sulfone era. Dr. T. F. Davey describes some of this
work in Nigeria: "A detailed account is given of the course of leprosy
in a group of very heavily infected villages in Eastern Nigeria between
the years of 1941 and 1956. Conditions for observation were exceptionally favorable. Three surveys in 1941, 1947, 1955 provided an
exact evaluation of the situation at those times. Cooperation of a high
order on the part of the people enabled the course of the disease
under the impact of various influences coming to bear upon it, to be
followed year by year. Possible causes for the rapid and great decline
in the disease which started in 1944 are discussed. The results of a
recent tuberculin survey make it extremely unlikely that tuberculosis
had any part in it. A lepromin survey has shown that in 1957 the level
of the positive reactors is still not high, and the natural evolution of
the disease is unlikely to have been an important factor. Deaths and
removal among leprosy patients may have had a small influence, as
may improvements in personal and public hygiene. Nevertheless leprosy control measures, made effective by great cooperation of the people, appear to have been the decisive factor. Treatment hindered the
development of lepromatous leprosy. Simple methods of isolation removed open cases from overcrowded communities. The follow-up of
contacts, discharged patients, and newcomers into the district, together with periodic surveys maintained public concern, and together
those measures effectively interrupted the course of the epidemic." In
spite of this experiment or work being one of the largest for a given
area, and in spite of using all known facts to reach the goal of reducing
the prevalence of leprosy, after the thirty years of work, in Eastern
Nigeria, in 1961 there were over a thousand new cases of leprosy
recorded. There is no doubt that there is much less advanced and
crippling leprosy than ever before in this area but the answer to the
eradication of leprosy has not been found.

The Treatment Control Centers or Clinics of Thailand are treating the highest number of actual leprosy cases of any single place in the world. Dr. Miguel reports the methods being used. In 1950 Thailand was really doing practically nothing as a government in its attempt to deal with leprosy control (though the government had three rather large colonies of two hundred to five hundred patients each). Now in conjunction with WHO there are over seventy thousand registered cases in the northeast of Thailand (population of the northeast about eight million). After eight years of control work, the difficulties are becoming more evident. It is quite clear that these clinics will never eradicate leprosy in Thailand.

Summary of Treatment Control Clinics

The important features of a Treatment Control Clinic program are, first, a survey of the population is made and at least 95 to 98 per cent of the actual number of cases of leprosy must be seen and examined. This examination includes the charting of the leprosy case. A record of all contacts is also made. Second, from 70 to 90 per cent of all cases found should be placed under treatment and kept there for five to twenty years.

As to whether infectious cases should be isolated until the bacterial index is negative is now under discussion by various authorities. Financially it is quite impossible for most countries. Psychologically it would be very difficult for Thailand. If half or less only of the contagious cases can be isolated, the larger group being free to infect the susceptibles with whom they come in contact, why penalize by isolation those who are willing to cooperate? Finally who is so wise today as to say just which ones are the dangerous cases and which are not?

Ruling out the expense and difficulty of getting sufficient adequately trained, conscientious paramedical workers, there are grave weaknesses with each of the first two steps of the Treatment Control Program which have been revealed during the years. In taking a census, one must expect to spend two years in order to complete a given area that is just large enough for one man to cover. In other words, frequent visits to a village are necessary to actually see every person in the place. An excellent idea of the total number of leprosy patients can be had by seeing 60 to 70 per cent of the total population and asking questions about the remainder, but to really eradicate leprosy from an area we must see and examine every person in every village. Contacts must be carefully recorded and regularly re-examined. This type of thing the average paramedical worker is not fully trained to do.

In Thailand a general clinic is being conducted in an area where careful survey work has been done and rechecked by WHO and yet in one year's time some forty cases of leprosy have come to our clinic (and they are coming one to three new cases every week) most of whom did not know they had leprosy and were missed by the survey. The second step, that of treating a large percentage of the leprosy cases long enough to really arrest the leprosy, is even more difficult than doing a complete survey. From 30 to 50 per cent of all cases stop regular treatment before the end of five years. In our general clinic we see a number who have done this. In the leprosy which we control we have found this to be universally true. What is to be done about this is hard to say. Certainly much more publicity as to the dangers of leprosy and the necessity of long treatment would be helpful. A mild law giving leprosy workers the power to enforce treatment in certain cases would jack up the morale of those wavering between treating and stopping. It is our opinion that the giving out of certificates of arrest or cure works against rather than for the eradication of leprosy. To be sure, the patient who receives the certificate is very happy but too many of these people accept it as proof that they will never have to take the medicine again. When a relapse occurs they are either too discouraged or too ashamed to take the medicine again until the disease has progressed far more than it needs to. A certificate of noninfectiousness may be given if necessary but all patients should be made to realize that medicine should be taken many years after they are apparently well. If the proper foundation is laid when the patient first begins treatment there will be no psychological letdown later on. It is true that wherever treatment clinics are placed within four to ten kilometers of all areas where there are leprosy cases a definite improvement of the situation takes place. More leprosy is observed, less crippling takes place. However, it has not yet been shown that there will be marked lowering of the prevalence of leprosy after ten years of trial. Most of us working with clinics feel there will be a gradual reduction in the total number of cases after ten to twenty years, but it is a real question if this type of control will eradicate leprosy even after fifty years of clinic treatments.

Leprosy Villages

There is another method of control which has been tried in small areas which combines some of the features of the colony and some of the features of a clinic, but avoids two of the inherent bad features of both. First and foremost it is the most economical method of leprosy work known. Second, it restores to the leprosy patient his ego, his sense of being somebody who can do something. The concentration of leprosy patients in villages offers the most economical form of leprosy control available. If properly developed it provides the benefits of the colony without its expense, it attracts the patient while the colony usually is feared by the large majority of those suffering with leprosy. It offers the essential benefits of clinics but is free of some of the difficulties inherent in clinics. These difficulties are, one, the necessity of patients traveling long distances to attend the clinic; two, the necessity of large numbers of paramedical workers for clinics; third, the cost is also much less than clinic work. Dr. Davey tells about villages which with a little more planning could have been just such type of leprosy village as we are about to describe. He says: ". . . a central outpatient clinic was opened, at which every patient found on the survey was enrolled. . . . Close to the clinic an isolation village of advanced hygienic pattern was built, sufficient in size to accommodate all open cases and such others as needed ulcer dressings or other medical attention. A patient-nurse was sent to live there, and soon gathered around him a nucleus of patients which grew rapidly. There were offered, to patients willing to isolate themselves, special farming privileges around this village." From my own limited observations, in Africa leprosy village formation would be easier than in many countries.

Thirty years of personal experience with leprosy villages—and added to this, twenty more years of records of villages existing before our experience began—have resulted in observations which convinced us that the leprosy village answers some of the problems which have made the other two methods unsatisfactory in the control of leprosy over large areas. In 1955 we wrote a summary of "the value of leprosy villages in a program of prevention"; also in a special letter in answer to Dr. Dharmendra's letter we supported the village values. During the years that have passed our opinions have been strengthened that the leprosy village is very valuable and objections to it should not deter us from the development of these villages. One very intelligent non-leprosy worker but well-trained medical man said, "Why has no village development occurred in important countries vitally interested in leprosy control?" Without going into detail one could simply reply, "Because they do not know the value of them." For twenty-five years we have emphasized the little value (compared with tremendous costs and small results obtained) of leprosy colonies. Many have felt this was not right and that we were destroying the basis of the only known way of controlling infectious types of leprosy. Now the attitude of epidemiologists is that colonies have not given us the results needed to control leprosy. As places for study and training and surgical operations they still are necessary though expensive parts of the total program. It might be said that though plastic surgery is a tremendous publicity agent for gaining recognition and finances, except for drop feet and restoration of the ability to close the eyes, most operations on the hands have not resulted in any change of occupation of the patient or improvement in his ability to earn more money. Many are the patients having hand surgery who are left no better than before and some often in worse condition. This is an argument not against hand surgery but for better and longer training of the average doctor who needs to do this type of surgery—which is a point emphasized by Dr. Paul Brand but often not appreciated.

Dr. Dharmendra in his dissenting letter concerning the leprosy villages of Kengtung, Burma, says: "In Burma, I found the state authorities responsible for antileprosy work looked upon these villages with great displeasure, since they considered them responsible for spreading the disease in surrounding parts." Neither Dr. Dharmendra nor the state authorities had ever been within two hundred miles of these villages. It is granted that they are considered responsible for spreading the disease in surrounding parts—but this is just the point, they are not responsible for spreading leprosy. The study made of three villages all within a diameter of thirty miles of one another as reported in 1955 showed that from all available evidence there was no contact spreading of leprosy from cases in these villages. This is particularly true of leprosy villages bordering directly on well villages as well as the villages situated some distance from other villages. It is a usual assumption by trained leprosy workers, and especially by government officials encumbered with the work of the leprosy problem of their area, that accumulations of leprosy patients near well villages are a dangerous thing. This is not proven when a careful study of the actual situation is made. It is somewhat similiar to our past assumption that children were the main source of new cases and that bacteriologically positive lepromatous cases were the main reservoir from which new cases were infected. Long-time study of the statistics point in the opposite direction. Continued study of leprosy villages during the past eight years has revealed no evidence that these leprosy villages are a source of spreading this disease, but on the contrary they seem to be an excellent method of halting the spread of leprosy in a given area.

It is unfortunate that the leprosy villages of Kengtung, Burma, cannot be studied more carefully. Political conditions of that area of the world make this impossible. In spite of the lack of trained personnel supervision, the leprosy villages continue to exist. Instead of disintegrating when financial help has largely been abandoned and only a part of needed medicine can be given due to transportation problems, this work has grown from nine hundred and fifty inmates in nine leprosy villages to over fourteen hundred in twelve villages. If political conditions allowed and the government gave the support it did before the war, one could hope that the total number of leprosy cases in the state of Kengtung would be cared for at a cost easily supported by the government.

In Northeast Thailand, due primarily to lack of vision on the part of either the government, WHO, or the missions, very little work has been done toward the development of leprosy villages. An outstanding Treatment Clinic Program is underway and perhaps it is best to have only one form of prevention program going on at one time until all are fully persuaded that it cannot eradicate leprosy in this area. There have been a few small villages started, one of them entirely at the instigation of two ambitious leprosy cases. With outside encouragement leprosy villages could become a large enough venture so that their value or failure could be assessed after ten more years.

In the north of Thailand, where the originally studied villages revealed so much pertinent information, the work still continues. It is a little stronger than eight years ago but could be a real factor in the lowering of the prevalence of leprosy in the north. Because of the length of time these villages have been in existence it offers an excellent field for further study of the value of such leprosy work. Unfortunately for the north, the McKean Leprosy Colony and the villages have such fame in the rest of Thailand that many cases of leprosy migrate from southern Thailand to the north for treatment and help.

Village Work of Robert Wulff

Outstanding for this type of work has been the work of Mr. Robert Wulff. Seeing the value of this type of village for the psychological benefit to the leprosy patient, he was convinced of the importance of the leprosy villages. In this type of surroundings the leprosy patient is happier than any other type. The other inmates of the village have the same sickness as he; persecution therefore disappears. If by chance a nonleprosy patient chooses to live in the village, he does so by the permission of the sick and he must live according to the standards of this village. Mr. Wulff, in order to better understand the problems involved and to wholeheartedly suggest better methods of living together, gathered some nine leprosy cases, all of whom were willing to work that they might have freedom, and went into the jungles, two kilometers from the main road beside a good stream of water. They literally hacked out plots of ground for their houses and gardens. As time passed, others who were willing to work joined the group. Pieces of land were allotted to the newcomers. Rice was given the patients until their gardens began to yield. This took from one to three years. Five years later what was the picture? Over one hundred and fifty patients had joined the group. Rice culture was unwise for these people. Instead they had over one hundred thousand banana plants; some sixty thousand high-grade pineapple plants; each had a small vegetable garden. Many learned to carve. Most important the village had a very high economic level. The young women of neighboring villages came to this village to seek husbands, in spite of the possible crippling of the men. From our preconceived need of keeping well people away from leprosy patients this seemed out of line, but from the economics of the situation it was a good thing to have more able-bodied people to work in the gardens, bring in rice, and perform other tasks requiring a lot of walking. From such records as we have of other villages of over twenty years' duration there is no evidence of leprosy spreading by the normal daily business mingling of villagers in these leprosy villages. It is a fact that children of leprosy patients should be more susceptible than the general run of children, and these susceptible children would certainly get leprosy if nothing were done to care for the leprosy parents. In the leprosy village patients are given DDS regularly and all children receive prophylactic medication. After some ten years of observation, children in these villages taking DDS have not developed leprosy. There has not been time enough or large enough series of cases studied to say there will be none. Such evidence as we have is encouraging. The work which Mr. Wulff did has so attracted lay people (doctors, as a rule, without facts to substantiate their prejudices are very cool to this project) that plans were made to establish two more such villages within a period of two years. From our experience, to go out and deliberately plan to establish villages for cripples and put a time limit on the job is almost asking the impossible. However, he accepted the challenge and two other villages on the same general plan have been developed. Because of the lack of interest of the medical profession the program has been taken out of medical circles and placed in the sphere of public welfare. This is as it should be, for the problems are 80 to 95 per cent those of public welfare rather than public health. However, from the available information it would seem wise for the Department of Health to utilize the Department of Welfare in order to further the solving of the up-to-the-present-unsolvable problem of the control and eradication of leprosy.

Details of a Leprosy Village

What do we mean by a leprosy village, how are they established, and what are the objections and difficulties involved? By a leprosy village we mean a group of leprosy patients who live together in a village exactly as do the people of that area. The village, we have learned from experience, must have twenty or more people making it up (in order that there may be a varied group, some are carpenters, one or more a blacksmith, the group is also needed for group ventures such as building houses, planting and reaping crops, and general protection) or else the village will disintegrate.

How do we go about establishing villages? First the need of villages must be apparent from the known prevalence of leprosy in the area. These villages may be three kilometers apart (due to natural development of some of the villages) or they may be one hundred kilometers apart. Ideally there should be about fifty kilometers between each village. This allows all within an area to come to it and know about it. The local customs often differ sufficiently in one hundred kilometers' distance so that leprosy patients might not feel happy or at home in the far-off areas. We recognize that many patients travel hundreds of miles to get care in a place from which they have heard good reports.

The village grows slowly. Three or four families make up the first group. Usually within six to twelve months one to ten more families will join if conditions are favorable. By favorable conditions we mean a little help is given temporarily such as thatch to help build a house and rice for a few months or a year. The less that is offered usually the slower the growth. The fewer the rules the happier is the whole situation. The rules that are needed are those common to all villages. These villages should have government approval but as far as possible not under direct government support. If supported by the government they become too heavy a burden for the budget, especially when fifty to one hundred or more villages are contemplated. Expense for these villages can be self-limited. Medicine is supplied free and there will be no taxes. Except for this, the village exists exactly like all villages of the same area. Herein lies the happiness of the leprosy patient. He can prosper by hard work or he can sit and do nothing and go hungry. He is not persecuted and he lives as he would if he were not sick. He is his own boss. No attempt is made to prevent well people from living in the village, although as a rule the well persons are relatives of a leprosy person in the village. In fact it is expected from past experiences that if an adequate number of villages are developed, so that leprosy patients from distant parts do not need to come to this section for needed care, by the end of fifty years leprosy will die out in these villaged areas. This has happened in the north of Thailand in less than forty years. A small staff can supervise five to one hundred villages looking after one to five thousand patients. Central hospitals can be developed probably by the government for research, teaching, surgical operations, and emergency medical care. It is important to emphasize that such central hospitals are not essential to the control of the spread or eradication of leprosy.

To establish a village after knowing the needs, one does a lot of talking with the patients and local officials. Every detail has to be gone over several times with those involved, concerning the need of the village and the location to be utilized. Fundamental to all this is that land must suit the people who will live there. Water supply is the primary consideration adequate for irrigation wherever possible. If at all in doubt one should wait the final decision until one dry season has passed. Personal observations made at that time will give the right answer. Another consideration: is adequate land available, is it land on which crops can be raised? It is not necessary that large tracts be had at once so long as it can be obtained later on. Some villages have started on the property belonging to one interested family, and from then on, as the need developed, more adjacent property was obtained.

The next step is official sanction. In this case, start as high up as possible. Once the proper top official has approved the over-all plan, minor officials at most are only a temporary nuisance. We do not ignore the minor official; in fact we do our best to enlist his support. This is where especially gifted assistants are worth their weight in gold. It has been our good fortune to have certain men at our disposal who could talk with officials, calm ruffled dispositions, or break down seemingly impossible obstacles. Experience is a great help in these matters.

Difficulties Associated with Village Work

In certain countries and areas it may be said that land is impossible to get. We would like to emphasize the fact that where there is a will there is a way. If there is leprosy in an area, a place for the patients to live must and can be found. In some countries the leprosy laws make leprosy villages legally impossible; then the first job may be to have the law changed. In six different countries where we have worked, ways and means to establish villages were found as soon as the workers were persuaded of the need.

Objections to leprosy villages by neighboring villages can be expected but once a village has been in existence for two to three years persecution will cease. This is why general approval of these villages should be had from the top officials. There is much the same kind of opposition to isolated leprosy people who live in or near a well village. Once a leprosy person has lived in a place for a period of time he becomes accepted and nothing is done to remove him. The difference between the isolated case and the leprosy village is that all the usual needs of people in the leprosy village are contained within the village. They have their own water supply, and can join together for mutual help. When the isolated leprosy case needs anything he is forced to seek it from well neighbors.

Begging is opposed and rightly so. This cannot be controlled 100 per cent in the first generation, but village morale and general opinions will slowly overcome it. Just telling a beggar not to beg will cure nothing; once his natural pride is gone he will continue to beg where prospects are good. The psychology conditioned in a beggar is almost impossible to eradicate. Only when begging becomes unprofitable will it stop. Finally, beggars are not a public-health menace. Leprosy is not spread by beggars; they are quite isolated at night and even on the streets do not make such contacts as would result in the spread of leprosy. Begging is primarily a public-welfare problem.

There is objection to the inmates of leprosy villages traveling into nearby villages and markets. Our findings in the three villages studied in the north of Thailand revealed no contact leprosy cases over a twenty-year period. This fear of contagion in the case of leprosy cannot be proved or justified by statistical study.

There are difficulties in starting a village. Often the patients for whom you are trying to do so much will not cooperate. One wants the village in one place, another wants it in quite a different location. One wants fields to cultivate, one wants bullocks and a cart, another wants pigs, etc. This is a matter of persuasion over a period of years. Others who are persecuted will drift into the village. Those who want help and see how well those in the villages are doing will come to live there. Disciplinary problems are handled the same as such problems are handled in any village of that particular area. Perfection is not expected but law and order is maintained.

Value of Philanthropic Agencies

Philanthropic organizations and various welfare groups are best suited to village work. Economically they can do more work over the years with less tax money than can the government. It is usually an impossible thing from the point of view of the budget for a government to do all the leprosy work needed to be done, whether it be clinics, colonies, or villages. The government should plan the successful control program but a part of its plan must be to utilize various agencies in fulfilling these plans. In this way tax money goes twice as far and the leprosy people receive more attention—kindly attention. Psychologically the philanthropic groups have more mercy and thoughtfulness for these unfortunate persons. Doctors are needed for general medical help, but the major problems are social and mental, for which most doctors are not properly equipped. Therefore administrators and religious leaders make the best leprosy workers for organizing villages and persuading both patients and officials of the right things to be done.

The importance of leprosy villages in a control program is emphasized by the following points: First, they are permanent. Second, no matter what the budget of the country is, no matter what the political trends may be, no matter if all assistance—technical, professional, or financial—fails, the village will remain. At any time special medicines or other newly discovered types of food or mode of life might be found helpful in the control of leprosy, it can be used in the leprosy village at once. Third, if there are certain people who prefer to attend clinics regularly these villages serve as excellent clinic centers. Most of the work of the clinic can be turned over to intelligent people within the village. They work for less salary; they are more reliable and are not seeking raises in salary or rank. They are acceptable to the people with whom they work. Supervision by well-trained paramedical workers is all that is needed.

Summary

The primary reason for leprosy programs is to do something that will eradicate leprosy. Many are the important things carried on in such programs which of themselves do not lead to the control of leprosy. Most of the operations and physiotherapy are of this nature. In the field of research we hope to learn things which can be used to improve our methods of control.

Three methods have been tried in the leprosy control programs. One has been the colony or sanatorium or home. A second is the Treatment Control Clinic usually preceded or accompanied by intensive surveys. A third method is the leprosy village. The leprosy village is the least known, the least used, and has no general approval. Analysis of the actual success of each of these methods shows that colonies have failed. Treatment Control Clinics are of value in lowering the number of cripples and the number of advanced lepromatous cases. To date, due to the expense of carrying on with large-scale efforts, or having an inadequate number of trained workers, or being unable to persuade a sufficient percentage of the cases to take medication for the proper number of years, this method has not brought the results that had been hoped for it. The leprosy village proves to be most economical; it can be adapted to budgets of varying amounts. The village once established will continue indefinitely regardless of political, financial, or other changing trends of the day.

Evidence accrued from the study of villages of twenty or more years' duration show no contact cases except in children of patients who lived before the DDS era. Villages which continue over thirty to forty years and where immigration from distant areas can be prevented will lose their leprosy stigma and no more leprosy cases will exist. This we have seen in the north of Thailand.

From the available facts we urge that those interested in the control and eradication of leprosy establish many villages to care for the leprosy patient until leprosy disappears in that area.

BIBLIOGRAPHY

Buker, R. S. "Note on Leprosy Villages in Burma." *International Journal of Leprosy* XXI, 1953.

—— "The Value of Leprosy Villages in a Program of Prevention." *International Journal of Leprosy* XXIII, 1955.

Cochrane, Robert G. *Leprosy in Theory and Practise.* Williams & Wilkins Co., Baltimore, 1959.

Davey, T. F. "Decline of Leprosy in a Group of Nigeria Villages Between 1941–1956." *International Journal of Leprosy* XXV, 1957.

Dharmendra, Letter to Editor. *International Journal of Leprosy* XXII, 1954.

Quarterly Public Health Reports—Eastern Nigeria—1960.

Wardekar, R. V. Fourth Report of the Gandhi Memorial Foundation, September 11, 1958. Wardha, Maharashtrar, India.

—— Personal Communications.

H47

		DATE DUE	